ENDOľ

With so much talk of "church :
dark days, it is refreshing to read
"estates" in the way of Luther's Si
produced a delightfully engaging book on Chirıs..
royal priesthood of believers that is both theologically deep and reau..,
accessible to all. This is a must-read for all who desire to let the light of
Christ shine in church, home, and society.

— REV. WILLIAM M. CWIRLA, PASTOR EMERITUS

The Rev. Dr. Espinosa has done the church a tremendous service in
producing a winsome, inspiring, and penetrating work on the often
misunderstood topics of sanctification and good works. Too many
books on this topic end in either a fruitless pursuit of self-absorbed
spiritual navel-gazing or a legalistic enterprise ultimately leading to
pride or despair. Espinosa offers readers a biblical and stimulating
alternative as he presents the Christian life as one lived within both a
Christological and a sacramental context as the baptized serve others in
Christ as they see Christ in the family, the church, and the state.

— REV. DR. STEVE PARKS,
ASSISTANT PROFESSOR OF THEOLOGY, CONCORDIA UNIVERSITY IRVINE

We Lutherans shine in expositing the faith to our fellow believers
but do not train our people on how to communicate to "outsiders."
How are we equipping our people to speak to today's young "nones"?
Exactly how would one conclude that a given religion was true?
How would one argue that a given religion was false? Today most
Westerners don't believe the Bible. So, we just say, "But our affirma-
tions are true and theirs are not." And even that answer draws forth a
response: "And how exactly do you know yours are true and theirs are
false?" The Rev. Dr. Espinosa has written a book that will be of genuine
help to Lutherans. Lutheran readers will profit by his careful exposition of subjects they will recognize if they were well catechized. As is so
common in western Protestant churches today, the emphasis is on the
Christian life (transformation, sanctification, etc.), but Rev. Espinosa
devotes one key section to the doctrine of justification, bless him!

I heartily recommend that Lutherans avail themselves of the
Rev. Dr. Espinosa's latest book.

— REV. DR. ROD ROSENBLADT,
PROFESSOR EMERITUS, CONCORDIA UNIVERSITY IRVINE

Dr. Espinosa explores the light of the world, the light of Jesus Christ, which, through the faithful baptized, shines through all interactions and serves all people. In every vocation given us by God, Espinosa explores how we might be devoted to service and love. The book assists those who counsel as it asks and answers the difficult questions about how the light of Jesus shines boldly through us in each of our vocations. Helpful questions at the close of each chapter, designed to invite reflection and discussion, make the book an excellent choice for a group study. This book will be a valuable asset for pastors and laity seeking a clear and faithful resource on the faithful, light-shining role of the humble Christian servant in each of the three estates.

— Dr. Beverly Yahnke, Executive Co-director,
DOXOLOGY: The Lutheran Center for Spiritual Care and Counsel

Christians in Europe and the US are facing difficult times. Here in Germany, the motherland of the Reformation, Christianity is no longer the majority. In such a climate, sharing Christ's love becomes a struggle. In *Faith That Shines in the Culture*, Dr. Espinosa does a marvelous job encouraging us not to give up hope. Again and again, he demonstrates how our identity rests in Christ. We are merely reflectors of His light. With many heartwarming, sometimes very humorous, examples from his personal and pastoral experience, Pastor Al demonstrates in a down-to-earth manner how God uses our daily vocations as parents, children, coworkers, citizens, and church members to share Christ's love with others. A valuable resource for Christians in the US and Germany alike.

— Pastor Simon Volkmar,
Church of the Great Cross, Hermannsburg, Germany

"You are the light of the world." These are wonderful words of promise from Jesus, but what exactly does He mean? Christians have wrestled with this question ever since Jesus first spoke these words. I am grateful that Rev. Espinosa has also grappled with this question and has given us a faithful and practical exposition of how the Christian faith shines in our culture through our daily life. As a pastor, I am especially thankful this vital topic is presented in a way that lends itself to group study. This is a most helpful resource, encouraging us all to let our faith shine wherever Christ has placed us.

— Pastor Darrin Sheek,
Prince of Peace Lutheran Church, Anaheim, California

FAITH THAT SHINES
IN THE CULTURE

Jesus Calls
Christians to Live
in the Family,
the Church,
and the State

ALFONSO ESPINOSA

CONCORDIA PUBLISHING HOUSE · SAINT LOUIS

DEDICATION

To my sister, Susan Marie Chavez, and brothers,
Lawrence Daniel Espinosa and Robert Rodney Espinosa

—and—

to my grandchildren since the last book:
Lucas and Maleah

ACKNOWLEDGMENTS

This book is about vocation taking place within sacred estates. In my own life, those servants of God true to their God-given vocations, helping me in family, church, and state, have profoundly impacted me. My parents of sacred memory, Robert and Josephine Espinosa, taught me that "if you have your family, you're rich." They were a fountainhead of rich blessing indeed. My siblings, Larry, Robert, and Susan, spoiled me, the youngest, with special attention and wisdom for life. My teachers and professors I could not have done without. In college, it was Rev. Dr. Charles Manske and Rev. Dr. Garth Ludwig—both in heavenly glory—who inspired me, as well as the Rev. Dr. Rod Rosenbladt, who still does. He is a blessed professor I am still able to consult with. In seminary, it was Rev. Dr. Dean Wenthe, Rev. Dr. David P. Scaer, and Rev. Kurt Marquart (now in heaven) who especially formed me theologically. Afterward, countless new professors, my doctoral supervisor Dr. Marius Felderhof (University of Birmingham, England), colleagues, fellow pastors, coworkers in the parish, and my gifted parishioners over the years, as well as my children and grandchildren, all have blessed me so that I might serve better in my vocations. Caring for my soul along the way have been my two father confessors: Rev. Robert Dargatz and Rev. Dr. Timothy Seals.

The 350+ footnotes represent the blessing of those whom I have cited to bolster and substantiate my writing for this volume. Some of those citations were through personal interviews. For these, I especially thank the executive director of Lutherans For Life, Rev. Michael Salemink; Dr. Todd Martin; attorney-at-law Tom Garrett; corporate executive Steve Furbacher; Rev. Dr. Timothy Seals; AA and Al-Anon experts George and Joni "B" (as I must refer to them in this volume); actress Lynn-Holly (Johnson) Givens; university provost Rev. Dr. Scott Ashmon; missionary Britt Odemba; and director of human care and ministerial support and advocate Dcs. Dr. Tiffany Manor. These brothers and sisters in Christ extend invaluable insights for this journey through sacred vocation in the various estates.

Dr. Russell P. Dawn, president of Concordia University Chicago, did more than write a gracious foreword for this book; he was also one I interviewed for a prior book. During that interview, Dr. Dawn set a fire in me about how the political sphere (within the state) is overshadowing the family and church estates. I knew in that instance that I had to start laying the groundwork that led to this volume. I thank him for his inspiration. As for the actual production, I wish to thank Jon and Veronica Steele for building the best workstation I've ever had. The motorized adjustable desk, the very large new screen, and overall lighting put me in a position to write most efficiently. Denise Seaman and Kiu Geisler are gifts from heaven. Denise has tackled for me—once again—the challenging task of collecting copyright permissions for many of the volumes I cite. Kiu has—once again—used her eye for detail to ensure my footnotes and bibliography are in accord with *The Chicago Manual of Style*. Mr. Shane Perry made my vision come to life through his tremendous gift of art. His early depictions of what the vertical call looks like streaming down to our horizontal calls within the major estates was a handle for my writing. Elizabeth Snyder, my eldest daughter, helped refine the cover design and is responsible for the ombre effect. My colleague Rev. Mark Jasa reminded me of the wonderful C. S. Lewis reference of the celebrated lady in heaven in *The Great Divorce*. Dr. Cari Chittick provided guidance on terminology for my chapter on singleness. All these colleagues remind me of the boundless blessings from the fellowship of the saints.

I am also grateful for the tremendous team at Concordia Publishing House. My experience from my first book in 2018 to the second in 2021 and now to this one in 2023 has been surrounded by gifted and talented servants of God in the Kingdom, dedicated to giving glory to Jesus and meaningful resources to God's people in the Church and those the Lord also loves who might be seeking and considering the sacred faith. I give thanks to my congregation, St. Paul's Lutheran Church of Irvine. They are the flock of Christ I am joyful to serve. They have been tremendously supportive of me writing while serving full-time in the parish. Their support reflects my congregation's attitude that our service in the Kingdom is not just for our local community but is a ministry that extends to the several missionaries we support and also to all who might receive the ministry I conduct through writing. Finally, no one has blessed me more than my wife, Traci Dawn. This book wouldn't exist without her. She granted permission for the very personal story I share in this book about us. She granted that permission because her attitude is one of service to others. She is not in vocations for herself. She gets it. It's about our neighbors, the ones we are called to love and to serve.

TABLE OF CONTENTS

FOREWORD

There are three things the reader ought to know about the author. The first is that he is the Rev. Dr. Alfonso Espinosa. Everything about him that ought to be serious is indeed very serious. The second is that he is known to all as Pastor Al. Everything about him that ought to be warm and approachable is deeply warm and approachable. The third and most important thing to know about him is that he is, to the greatest extent I have seen in any person, always both parts of the dichotomy. When you interact with him, you are getting the serious-minded Rev. Dr. Espinosa and you are equally getting the warm Pastor Al. Unsurprisingly, you will find that to be true as you engage with *Faith That Shines in the Culture*. Every page is serious and every page approachable.

I met Pastor Al in a high school gymnasium in 2012. My family and I had just moved to Irvine, California, and we were looking for a church. St. Paul's Lutheran Church of Irvine was at that time holding services in the gymnasium of a local Lutheran high school. What we found when we visited was a preacher who preached with theological precision about our need of a Savior and the love of God in Christ Jesus, our Savior, and did so with engaging passion. We found a liturgist who brought the full heritage of our Lutheran liturgy into that strange setting and did so with a completely natural air. We found a pastor who cared deeply about his flock, about welcoming newcomers, and quite simply about people. And finally, we found a congregation that perfectly fit this living paradox.

Pastor Al and I became friends and spent many hours serving, eating, and conversing together. Our families dined together, watched sports together, and even went to a Dodgers game together. More accurately, his family went to a Dodgers game and my family went to a Rockies game, and we all sat together in Chavez Ravine. He was my pastor, confessor, friend, advisor, and guide. He catechized my daughters. It is now four years since my family and I moved to River Forest, and he remains a trusted friend and advisor.

His importance to me matters to you, the reader, because this book simply exudes Pastor Al. All the seriousness and warmth that he bears, all the precision and approachability, all the pastoral application of abstract truth to lived experience—all these things are in the pages ahead.

What lies before you is a book on theology that does not read like a book on theology. When you arrive at the last page, your understanding will have grown, but you will feel like you just had an amiable conversation with Pastor Al. Besides being clear and accessible, the work feels caring. But it is not a soft-and-squishy sort of caring. It is more like the sober caring of a teacher who invites their students for a home-cooked meal and spends the evening listening to them and speaking wisdom into their lives and aspirations. This book on theology is personal.

The theology at the center of *Faith That Shines in the Culture* is the doctrine of vocation—that is, God's call to serve our neighbors. There are many books about vocation out there, a few of which are quite good. Where this work particularly shines (pun intended) is in its application of the doctrine to the three estates: family, church, and state. That framework is important, useful, and often neglected. In my own life, I have found that it helps to order my thinking, which in turn affects both what I do and how I perceive the world around me. To boil it down, the framework teaches that God calls every Christian to service in each estate, and although the service looks different in each estate, at the center of all such service is love for our neighbors. *Faith That Shines in the Culture* is a clear and personal walk through God's call to each of us to serve lovingly in the family, the church, and the state.

In true Pastor Al fashion, he begins and ends the book with Jesus, the Alpha and Omega. Also in true Pastor Al fashion, he is thorough and methodical, dissecting service in each estate systematically and from several angles. Of note, his chapter on God's call to some to live in the family estate of singleness is sorely needed in this cultural moment. More broadly, *Faith That Shines in the Culture* will help you to think more clearly about the life to which God is calling you. If you have ever pondered matters such as the difficulty of balancing work life and home life, why it is important that we gather when we worship, or whether our governments should be more forgiving, then you will find answers here.

Regardless of your path to this point, you, the Christian reader, will find yourself in these pages. More importantly, however, you will find the faith once delivered to the saints. Pastor Al would have it no other way.

RUSSELL P. DAWN, DPHIL, JD
PRESIDENT, CONCORDIA UNIVERSITY CHICAGO

PREFACE

There's an old country song called "Looking for Love in All the Wrong Places."[1] I was like that in respect to Christian sanctification (the new life in Christ that results from our being justified through faith in Christ). I was looking for the transformation that Christ brings in all the wrong places. My goal was to have an immediate and direct experience with the Holy Spirit. Little did I know that I was dabbling in the condition Luther described as someone having "devoured the Holy Spirit feathers and all."[2]

What was developing along the way was a tendency toward becoming increasingly self-absorbed. I started to imagine that the key to sanctification was inner experience: thoughts, desires, and pious visions that would allow me to check my progress. The more sanctification boxes checked, the better my spiritual temperature. This approach was unfortunately the regular occasion for pride as opposed to the very humility the Holy Spirit desires to create in us.

A real irony was taking place: my supposed confession as a Lutheran Christian had at its core trusting in the Gospel that I was saved from sin, death, and the power of the devil on account of Christ. Christ *came to* me. That is, salvation comes from the *outside* not the *inside*, but there I was returning to myself, to my inside.[3]

This problem becomes the oft repeated return to the Law. The Law of God of course is holy (Romans 7:12), but it must be used in the proper

---

1   Johnny Lee's song was released in June 1980 as part of the soundtrack to the film *Urban Cowboy*, which released that year.

2   AE 40:83, which references Luther's treatise entitled *Against the Heavenly Prophets in the Matter of Images and Sacraments* of 1525. Luther wrote against the "spiritualists" who had placed mysticism over the Word and Sacraments while compromising the real presence of Christ in the Holy Sacrament.

3   *Extra nos* ("outside ourselves") is crucial in orthodox, biblical Christianity. Salvation comes to us from outside of us in Christ.

way. When we begin to use it for our comfort and confidence, that's when we go astray. Instead, as a mirror reflects our faces, the Law reveals how much we need Christ since we fall short of God's Law.[4] The falling short part is a condition we can never overcome on this side of heaven.

The Christian, however, also *delights* in God's Law, but only in response to Jesus, who fulfilled the Law for us. In Christ we are led to love the Law of Christ, and the new man delights in keeping it—but not to be saved by it, because he is already saved in Christ. Thus, the Law always accuses, but it does not *only* accuse. The new man has a different relationship with the Law.

To willingly keep God's commandments and to consider them as not burdensome (1 John 5:3) occurs only after knowing the love of God and the saving Gospel of Christ. Even at that, however, we must return to the Law accusing us again so that we are always running back to Jesus, who graciously receives and never tires of forgiving us. This is a necessary cycle until we see Christ face to face.

But recall the problems of self-absorption and inward orientation when it comes to approaching the new life. Can the Christian remain outward oriented also regarding sanctification? Not only can we, but we are meant to be.

Our sanctification in Christ means we are now zeroed in on our neighbor and not ourselves. We approach others in Christ and see Christ in the ones in front of us. The Lord blesses us in this way to also keep our eyes off ourselves. In fact, we are freed up to forget about our spiritual temperatures and holy box-checking. Christ has set us free from sinful self-absorption. We can now live for God by living to love and serve our neighbors. When the Holy Spirit leads us to live this way, we are inherently and at the same time loving God.[5]

How does this new life come to be? It comes through the fact that Christians are *called* by God. How does the Christian know they are

---

4   *Lex semper accusat,* "the Law always accuses [or reveals our sin]."

5   1 John 4:21: "And this commandment we have from Him: whoever loves God must also love his brother."

called? By being baptized into Christ! This call from God is the article of the faith referred to as *holy vocation.*[6]

The most important call from God to a person is the call to become a Christian, born again by water and the Spirit (John 3:5). Holy vocation, therefore, is the new life that God calls into being to live as baptized-into-Christ children of God. This chief calling permeates our lives in everything we do as Christians. Jesus, the light of the world, in this way creates His Christians to be the light of the world. God shines through His people who are faithfully living in their holy call or holy vocation.

And this is true sanctification, and its outward direction not only protects our new lives but also helps our neighbor. When we are faithful to God's call to live in Christ, the neighbor experiences God serving them through us. This is how the light of Christ reaches people today. In this way, sanctification is not only immensely practical, but it becomes something we are not self-conscious about. True sanctification doesn't try to be sanctified. Instead, the Christian becomes preoccupied with his neighbor.

In respect to faith, we live in Christ. In respect to love, we live in our neighbor, even as Jesus identifies Himself as "the least of these my brothers" (Matthew 25:40). Thus, even in sanctification we live in Christ, who is also called our sanctification (1 Corinthians 1:30).

As a result of our chief calling and vocation, therefore, we are led to receive other callings (multiple vocations—plural—which flow from the chief vocation—singular). God is not willy-nilly about how we love our neighbors. The Lord calls us also into specific duties and stations in the world as arranged and designed by Him. We live out our several callings through God's estates, or realms, of family, church, and state.

In other words, our call from God to be a Christian is what we might call our *vertical* call—we are after all "born from above" (John 3:3)—and then our lives as Christians are played out in the world through our several *horizontal calls* serving our neighbor in the family,

---

6   From the Latin *vocare*, which means "to call," and what God calls becomes real. His call to belong to Him creates in people the new life in Christ.

church, and state.[7] Another way of stating this is to say that our chief call is Christ *upon* us (as in His light shining upon us) and our several callings are Christ *through* us (as in His light shining through us toward our neighbors).[8]

It is often observed that from the outside looking in, when it comes to living out our God-given vocations, that the actual work we do looks very much like what anyone does. Christians and non-Christians alike change diapers, go to work, spend time with friends, and live as citizens. What is often observed makes Christians and non-Christians virtually indistinguishable. For example, a good heart surgeon does not appear more Christian while performing effective open heart surgery.

Still, there must be some significance to the fact that Jesus calls His people *light*. How does the light of Christ shine through us in our daily callings? How does our primary calling as baptized people of God, the royal priesthood of God in this world, impact our several day-to-day callings? How is it that the light of Christ is intended to shine through His people living in the three realms of family, church, and state? How does the vertical call radiate upon and then through the horizontal ones? To answer these immensely important questions, I was compelled to write this book.

These questions, however, were not the first step toward how this book came about. God worked through someone that got me on this track to begin with. During the research for my second book, I had the privilege to interview Dr. Russell Dawn, president of Concordia University Chicago.

We were discussing engaging politics when Dr. Dawn presented the refreshing perspective that politics consists of human interactions within the three estates provided to us by God: the family, the church, and the state. Recall that *polis* refers to the *entire* ancient Greek city-state. And then Dr. Dawn said this:

---

7   "Born from above" is a superior translation to "born again" at John 3:3.

8   There is yet another call pertaining to the office of the holy ministry. This is for another book.

America's fundamental problem is that we have lost sight of the first two [estates]. As a result, there are those who want to make the state the entire realm . . . as the state encroaches upon family and church.[9]

I was deeply bothered by what Dr. Dawn had said even as I knew in my gut he was right. In our great land, the family and church are disintegrating before our eyes while matters of the state seem to permeate our headline news. This does not imply that God-established government that serves the state is not necessary. It *is* necessary (Romans 13:1–7). At the same time, it, too, will suffer unless the other two estates are properly maintained.

Christians, therefore, should be doing everything they can as good stewards to restore equilibrium to the three estates. This is not a power struggle, but an effort to get back to what our new lives are all about: serving our neighbors the best way we can. If any of the three estates suffer, people will too.

What then should Christians be doing? They can get back to a right application of their singular, vertical calling from God so that the light of Jesus might shine in all their horizontal callings lived out in all three estates. This book is an attempt to help Christians shine the light of Christ more brightly as they love their neighbors. In the process, we will see that God intends that Christian sanctification be about blessing the people around us. It's time for us to consider, and I hope embrace, *Faith That Shines in the Culture.*

---

9   Alfonso Espinosa, *Faith That Engages the Culture* (St. Louis: Concordia Publishing House, 2021), 124.

INTRODUCTION

RECEIVING AND REFLECTING CHRIST'S LIGHT

Receiving and Reflecting

Growing up, my mother was steadfast in reminding me that as I ventured out into the world, I was not only representing myself but also the entire family. A son might bring honor to his family, but he was also capable of bringing shame. If he spoke foolishly, then the societal response might be, "I guess his parents didn't teach him any better."[10]

Because I had received the family name, I would now reflect it as well. For good or for bad, I had no choice in the matter. My parents urged me to make good impressions, and I was glad to be able by the grace of God to make them proud.

As Christians, we understand this truism demonstrating that what we receive will lead to the reflection of what is now ours. We are like that stone splashing in the middle of a pond causing the radiation of concentric circles upon the water. The pond that receives the stone must reflect what has entered it. Similarly, Christians have received Christ, so we don't go out into the world only representing ourselves. Because we have received Christ, we now represent and reflect His entire Church and, more importantly, the fact that Christ is not just for Christians but for all people in the entire world.

This pattern is inevitable, whether we like it or not. Indeed, there really isn't anyone who is an island unto themselves. What we are impacts other people—either positively or negatively.

---

10   Josephine Zaragoza Espinosa, circa 1970s, Delano, CA.

Christ Received through Word and Sacraments

Christians know with certainty they have received and continue to receive the Lord Jesus Christ through His Word, taught or preached, through His poured-out Word in Holy Baptism, through His sacramental Word in Holy Communion, through His absolving Word in the corporate confession or private confession with the pastor, and through the mutual encouragement of Christians as they speak and apply Christ's Word to one another.[11]

To have such clarity about exactly when and where we are connected to Christ is fantastically important. God does not want us to doubt our connection to His Son, so our reception of Christ is not esoteric, doubtful, weird, or off in a corner. It is objectively experienced and verifiable. It is an empirical reception. It occurs in the real world and is perceived by real senses while being verified by real witnesses. He who has been baptized has received Jesus. There is no doubt about it, the one who has received Jesus will invariably reflect Jesus.

The Word Received Is Light, and Light Reflects

Let us consider more about the Lord Jesus received by Christians. The first record of Jesus speaking aloud in Holy Scripture is "Let there be light" (Genesis 1:3).[12] Now that's interesting. The first thing God called into existence was light. He called light out of nothing.[13] The scene at creation, however, is even more intriguing when we consider that Jesus identified as the Creator (John 1:1; Colossians 1:16) also described Himself in John 8:1, saying, "I am the light of the world. Whoever follows Me will not walk in darkness, but will have the light of life." Light created light. And He wasn't finished creating.

Jesus is not only the source and cause of created light, but He is Himself *the* light who gives the light of life to people. When anyone receives the light of Christ, that same person will demonstratively reflect

---

11   Smalcald Articles III IV.

12   The Church sees the Holy Trinity in the opening words of Genesis 1: "God" (the Father) at verse 1, the (Holy) Spirit at verse 2, and God speaking/The Word/Jesus Christ at verse 3.

13   The article of the Christian faith pertaining to creation is called *creatio ex nihilo*, or *creation out of nothing*. God required no primordial or preexisting material to create.

that light of Christ. We are not surprised, therefore, that the Lord Jesus also described His Church (all His people) this way: "You are the light of the world. . . . Let your light shine before others, so that they may see your good works and give glory to your Father who is in heaven" (Matthew 5:14, 16). Christians receive the light of Christ and reflect the light of Christ. Thus, the life of the Christian is to constantly receive Christ's light and to perpetually reflect it to others.

Let's be clear, this light reflected by Christians is not an ambiguous spiritual aura. David P. Scaer points out that the works referred to in Matthew 5 flow from the preaching of Christ and "are the works of mercy which Jesus also did among the people. These works thus bring the reality of the redemption [of Christ] into the world."[14] In other words, the light of Christ that brings life is empirical: His light shines when the Gospel of God's love and mercy for sinners is put into their mouths, upon their foreheads, and into their ears. These become the born-from-above ones who go on to reflect the works of Jesus by doing them continually until He comes again. Light generates the works of light.

The symbolism of light is powerful in demonstrating that God connects to His people to save them. John 1:4 says: "In [Jesus Christ] was life, and the life was the light of men." Craig R. Koester points out that God sends light, which "manifests the power and presence of God," while whoever receives light "manifests the 'life' given to people through God's Word."[15] The result is a new life that knows God through faith in Christ.[16] And this faith invariably leads to the new life entirely focused on serving the neighbor. New life is as a result reflected.

Walking as Children of Light

At the same time, our reflecting and manifesting Christ's light is not transient or something that comes and goes. Since the light is Christ, we are in Christ and Christ is in us. Christ is before us, beside us,

14   David P. Scaer, *The Sermon on the Mount: The Church's First Statement of the Gospel* (St. Louis: Concordia Publishing House, 2000), 98.

15   Craig R. Koester, *Symbolism in the Fourth Gospel: Meaning, Mystery, Community*, 2nd ed. (Minneapolis, MN: Augsburg Fortress, 2003), 143.

16   Koester, *Symbolism in the Fourth Gospel*, 143.

beneath us, within us, and above us. Again, He shines upon us and through us. And He, the light of the world, is given to and possessed by the Christian. Every time the Christian receives the Holy Sacrament of the Altar, the light enters their mouths and fills their lives.

St. John records Jesus speaking to His disciples: "While you have the light, believe in the light, that you may become sons of light."[17] The word *Christian* means "Christ's." The Christian *belongs* to Jesus Christ. She *has* Jesus and Jesus *has* her. Christians have the light, Jesus. What is His is now theirs.[18] This makes them sons of light.[19] Christians are heirs of light.

God guarantees that light is received by Christians as He and the Son have sent the Holy Spirit (John 14:26; 15:26; 16:7), working through the reverberating light that travels through airwaves and the elemental light that touches us through water, bread, and wine. God is saying to His people, "Don't doubt it. The light is *yours*."

These children of light live, move, and have their being in the light who is Christ. They *walk* as children of light.[20] "In ethical terms, the children of light were understood to be those who lived according to the will of God."[21] This life is especially seen when Christians live out Christ's command to love one another (John 13:34). And this love is to extend not only to the fellowship of Christians but also to all people in emulation of God's saving love for all (John 3:16).

Light Contrasts Darkness

Having received the light, we are not to sit around basking in it, feeling good about ourselves. Christians have serious work to do, and what an exciting privilege is ours to do what the Lord has called us to do.

Nevertheless, this work we are called to is vehemently resisted and often rejected by the world. John 1:5 states, "The light shines in the darkness, and the darkness has not overcome it." As a result, though

---

17   John 12:36

18   And what is theirs, namely their sin, becomes His, which He covered with His blood.

19   To be a "son" is to be an heir, male or female.

20   This verb is used in Scripture to describe how a person actively lives.

21   Koester, *Symbolism in the Fourth Gospel*, 165.

the world was made through Christ, the world did not know Him (John 1:10). Even many of His own people did not receive Him (John 1:11). William C. Weinrich maintains that this darkness "characterizes the world estranged from God and opposed to His will and therefore determined by death. As the present passage indicates [John 1:5] 'darkness' shows itself especially in opposition to Christ and to the life that He offers."[22]

Christians have faith in Christ, but the world does not. Christians love with God's love, but the world does not. We cannot pretend that God's Word doesn't maintain a serious difference among people. While our culture is agitated by this reality, God would use it to urge Christians to shine Christ's light upon those who do not know the grace of God through His Son. Because Jesus loves *all* people, Christians are sent by God to engage *all* people that they, too, would know the gift of eternal life.[23]

The light of Christ must also be continually shone upon those who already are Christians. Serving as a called pastor for over three decades in three different congregations and for many hundreds of God's people, I have had experiences that were all over the map. Pastors should never be surprised at how darkness will confront God's people, nor should they be surprised at how effective and healing the light of Christ is in overcoming darkness. Darkness cannot overcome the light, but the light overcomes the darkness. Pastors must proclaim and announce this with vigor and conviction because God's Word is true.

One parishioner was confronted by darkness to the extent that it was enveloping him and controlling his life. I had a chance to sit down with this precious lamb of Christ, this baptized one for whom Jesus had died for (covering his sin) and rose for (conquering his death). I came to him to give him Christ's Word and Sacrament. On this occasion, there was also a witness with us to help us pray.

I took time to teach first. Catechesis that conveys the light of Christ is to be a constant in the life of the Christian. It must be applied throughout

---

22   William C. Weinrich, *John 1:1–7:1*, Concordia Commentary (St. Louis: Concordia Publishing House, 2015), 145.

23   The present volume is the logical sequel to my book *Faith That Engages the Culture* (St. Louis: Concordia Publishing House, 2021).

the undulations we face when we are tempted to lose hope and when we think we are standing strong and every moment in between. We discussed the *struggle* St. Paul elaborates upon in Ephesians 6 and the full armor of God, which counters the ranks of demonic forces.[24] The baptized have a target on their backs, and they often feel the oppression of darkness. But the Lord gives light.

When we finished the study, I explained the liturgical prayer service I would lead using Luther's Small Catechism and, of course, the Word of God I had prepared. What we were about to do was apply the light of Christ to the darkness oppressing this baptized child of God. The core of the service included my hand upon my parishioner's head in prayer as I proclaimed the Word of Christ upon him.

This was no Hollywood drama. The faithful pastor puts Christ before the baptized and only Christ. During the service, I would recite a part of the catechism or the Word of God, and then I instructed my parishioner to repeat what I had just said.

We started. I declared, "In the name of the Father and of the Son and of the Holy Spirit. Amen." I told him to repeat the Invocation aloud. He said, "I can't." What I thought I heard was that he was afraid, or hesitant, or simply wouldn't, but I had misunderstood. I replied, "Of course you can. Repeat after me. (I spoke it again.) Do it." He was struggling—struggling so much, in fact, that a stream of sweat started down his temples while he trembled. "You don't understand, pastor, I am *unable, the words won't come out of my mouth.*" His despair was palpable.

I proclaimed what was true: "You cannot by your own strength, but *Christ* can through you. The evil one lies. You can do all things through Christ who strengthens you (Philippians 4:13). Now, repeat after me: 'In the name . . .'" (I paused as I would lead him one little step at a time).

He uttered, "In the name . . ." and then we were off and running. Every sentence was a struggle, but he was enabled to speak. We covered the entire Six Chief Parts of the catechism, and we confessed the truth of Christ's victory over sin, the world, and the devil. We then celebrated the Sacrament of the Altar.

---

24 Ephesians 6:10–20.

After a long time, my parishioner was drenched with sweat and exhausted. I instructed him to take some water and go to bed. He slept like a baby. It was the first time in a very long time he had been able to sleep like that. The next day, he realized a terrible weight had been lifted from him.

My parishioner still struggles like the rest of us. He will always on this side of heaven know the battle so clearly depicted in Romans 7 and Galatians 5, but he is living with a joy I didn't see before. He is excited to travel with the light of Christ, which first overcame his darkness at his Baptism but continues to do so through absolution, the Supper, and constant study of God's Word. The bottom line is this: the light of Christ overcomes our darkness.

Reflectors Who *Are* Light

Christians often neglect to think of themselves as becoming light in Christ. But we should soak in this gift more often: by virtue of having received Jesus Christ into our lives, we have been made His lights. We are His new creation (2 Corinthians 5:17), but we don't necessarily connect the dots for realizing the ramifications. Thomas M. Winger lays it out for us as he teaches about Ephesians 5:8, which says, "For at one time you were darkness, but now you are light in the Lord. Walk as children of light." Winger elaborates:

> Now they [Christians] are not simply *in* the light, but they *are* light, endowed with its qualities. . . . "Light" appears only in this pericope [in Ephesians] and a remarkable five times (5:8 [twice], 9, 13, 14). By their rebirth as sons of God (1:5), Christians have taken on the image of God (4:24), who is the light.[25]

Winger explains that to be light as Christians means specifically that we are in Christ—"Christlike"—and led by His Word.[26] And Ephesians 5:9 describes us now as producing fruit that is "good and right and

---

25   Thomas M. Winger, *Ephesians*, *Concordia Commentary* (St. Louis: Concordia Publishing House, 2015), 560. First two sets of brackets added.

26   Winger, *Ephesians*, 561.

true." Winger connects that which is good with our works, that which is right with our active and passive righteousness in Christ, and that which is true with Christ Himself and His Gospel.[27]

Philippians 2:15–16 is another verse in Holy Scripture that helps us to understand our new lives:

> That you may be blameless and innocent, children of God without blemish in the midst of a crooked and twisted generation, among whom you shine as lights in the world, holding fast to the word of life, so that in the day of Christ I may be proud that I did not run in vain or labor in vain.

Christians are to view themselves as R. C. H. Lenski described, as "luminaries in the world."[28] As if to predict our natural incredulity, Lenski goes on to say, "Even imperfect Christians shine; when Jesus spoke to His then very imperfect disciples He did not use the future tense . . . but the present: '*you are*' (Matthew 5:14)."[29] St. Paul did not make a simple assertion that Christians are luminaries but goes on to point out how this is so: they were, or are, "holding fast to the word of life."[30]

The interplay of Word and light is put forth in this Lutheran prayer by Johann Eichorn (ca. 1518–64), written for the Feast of the Epiphany (the first half):

> Lord God, heavenly Father, who have [sic] caused Your dear Word, the true star that shows us the infant Jesus, to shine on us: we beseech You to put Your Holy Spirit into our hearts, that we may receive that light and make salutary use of it.[31]

---

27   Winger, *Ephesians*, 562. Note: Christ's passive righteousness God declares upon us for Christ's sake; and Christ's active righteousness for us is Christ's life through us. As for active righteousness, consider, for example, John 15:5: "I am the vine; you are the branches. Whoever abides in Me and I in him, he it is that bears much fruit, for apart from Me you can do nothing."

28   R. C. H. Lenski, *The Interpretation of St. Paul's Epistles to the Galatians, to the Ephesians and to the Philippians* (Minneapolis, MN: Augsburg, 1937), 803.

29   Lenski, *St. Paul's Epistles*, 803.

30   Lenski, *St. Paul's Epistles*, 804.

31   Matthew Carver, trans., *Lutheran Prayer Companion* (St. Louis: Concordia Publishing House, 2018), 43.

God Wants Us to Shine in Darkness

Because of our sin-impacted way of thinking, however, we hesitate to think that *everyone* we know *should* receive God's light through us. Isn't it true that some people just don't deserve it? No, not good enough. What *is* true is that *no one* deserves it, including ourselves. And yet, God has given it to me, the worst of sinners.[32] Perhaps it is good after all that I might shine Christ's light on everyone else.

I've been blessed with eight children, five of whom are daughters. If there is anything in the universe that brings out the protective instinct in a father, it is a daughter. The five of them joined forces to help me grow an impressive salting of grey-silver hair. And while I would like to say that my hair color is simply indicative of sublime wisdom, the truth is far less impressive. My daughters are great and I'm crazy about them, but they became teenagers along the way and started dating. Need I say more?

One of the many courters who came under my roof to introduce themselves was a young man who just gave me the wrong vibe. I couldn't put my thumb on it, but something was off. I didn't trust him.

One fateful evening, however, my daughter met him behind my back. The young man became violent toward her, and I got there after the police arrived at the scene with my heart pounding out of my chest. What confronted me next was something I had never experienced. I never knew how anger could consume a soul as it began to take over my own.

The Lord knew what He was doing. Besides the fact that the event brought my daughter and me closer than we had ever been, the Lord taught me a lesson about the seriousness of forgiveness and the dark hole that can develop when forgiveness is withheld. I realized that as justifiably angry as I had become toward the young man, I could not forget the Lord's command: "Be angry and do not sin . . . and give no opportunity to the devil" (Ephesians 4:26–27). I had to give up the terrible sense of vindictiveness I was holding onto.

It was time for light to shine on the situation as I was led to get on my knees to confess the darkness in my soul. Then, the Lord blessed

---

32   I am implying that we emulate St. Paul's attitude in 1 Timothy 1:15.

me by permitting me to receive a phone call. It was time for the young man's court hearing, and my daughter and I were given a choice about the severity of charges we could press. We prayed together with clarity about the important role the sword of our government wields (Romans 13:4), mindful also of the help people can receive through measured consequences.

With this clarity and for this unique situation, my daughter and I were led to mercy and chose to press the lesser charge. In this case, I knew that our decision was, in fact, the fruit of the repentance the Lord had permitted to take place in me. At the same time, it was a way of shining light on yet another sinner like me. The young man received a dose of light. This is what God does. He shines light where there is only darkness, and the darkness has not and cannot overcome it.

Isaiah 9:2 anticipates the glorious revelation of the Messiah to everyone overcome in darkness: "The people who walked in darkness have seen a great light; those who dwelt in a land of deep darkness, on them has light shone." John N. Oswalt explains that the people who were once "groping in darkness . . . suddenly find themselves blinking in the light," and then he offers these beautiful words about God's grace: "So here, there is light for these people because their sin and rebellion are not enough to keep God from manifesting himself to them."[33]

That stress-invoking supervisor, that untrustworthy family member, that coworker who seems to specialize in testing your patience, that one in authority whom you trust as far as you can throw, that in-law who seems to put the worst construction on things just to irritate you, that classmate spreading false rumors, and that person who hurt your loved one—or directly hurt *you*—all these God has put in our lives that His light might shine upon them.

We underestimate why things are as they are. After all, if everyone else would just ascend to our level of insight, then we would all get along. Instead, the effects of sin are ubiquitous. Everyone who hurts

---

33   John N. Oswalt, *The New International Commentary on the Old Testament* (Grand Rapids, MI: William B. Eerdmans, 1986), 242.

us has been hurt. Every sinner who inflicts pain has been inflicted by pain. But the pervasiveness of the light of Christ is greater still.

Nevertheless, when people are in the thick of darkness, it is easy to feel as though all hope is gone. Isaiah 59:9 says, "Therefore justice is far from us, and righteousness does not overtake us; we hope for light, and behold, darkness, and for brightness, but we walk in gloom." But as R. Reed Lessing asserts, "It is therefore time for them to wake up, get out of bed, and rub the sleep out of their eyes."[34]

With these words, Lessing, of course, anticipates Isaiah 60:1–3:

> Arise, shine, for your light has come, and the glory of the Lord has risen upon you. For behold, darkness shall cover the earth, and thick darkness the peoples; but the Lord will arise upon you, and His glory will be seen upon you. And nations shall come to your light, and kings to the brightness of your rising.

Lessing is eloquent while reminding us, "Jesus is the Light of the world, who took on flesh so that he might take you into his arms, heal your hurts, forgive your filth, and destroy your darkness."[35] And this happens on account of God's call. Lessing reminds us that the imperative "shine" is not a mere admonition but a word of power.[36] Just as created light appeared at Jesus' command (Genesis 1:3), the light of new life in Christ appears whenever anyone receives Jesus' command to shine, that is, to share His light with all your neighbors. This *is* the new life we celebrate as we sing:

> Rise, shine, you people! Christ the Lord has entered
> Our human story; God in Him is centered.
> He comes to us, by death and sin surrounded,
> With grace unbounded.

---

34   R. Reed Lessing, *Isaiah 56–66*, Concordia Commentary (St. Louis: Concordia Publishing House, 2014), 239. Lessing also quotes Ephesians 5:14 in this context: "Awake, O sleeper, and arise from the dead, and Christ will shine on you."

35   Lessing, *Isaiah 56–66*, 240.

36   Lessing, *Isaiah 56–66*, 240.

Tell how the Father sent His Son to save us.
Tell of the Son, who life and freedom gave us.
Tell how the Spirit calls from every nation
His new creation. (*LSB* 825:1, 4)

How We Receive and Reflect: Call and Calls

We have already identified that it is the Holy Spirit, working through the Word and Sacraments of Christ, who brings the light of Christ to us and who shines the light of Christ through us, but the Word itself helps us to be more specific about this. The Holy Spirit connects us to the one-of-a-kind call (singular) of God that creates our new lives as children of light. This call is from above, and thus I refer to it as our *vertical* call, uniting us to Jesus Christ, the light of the world. Through this call, the light of Christ is put *upon* us.

Having received this chief and most important call, God then leads us to come into many calls (plural). In these calls, the light of Christ shines *through* us and what I refer to as our *horizontal* calls, putting us in a position to serve and love our neighbors through our many stations in life.[37]

I mentioned above that the actual work conducted by Christians with the light of Christ and non-Christians without this light (since light upon us indicates conversion and new life) can seem indistinguishable. Again, as mentioned, a good heart surgeon does not seem more or less Christian in the middle of heart surgery. However, there is more to the story.

A person—any person—is not a compartmentalized entity. Let us return to the example of the surgeon above. The surgeon is a surgeon wherever she goes, but there is more to her life than being in the middle of replacing an aortic valve. When surgery is over, she will interact with colleagues, check in with the patient post-surgery, represent the field of medicine, fulfill civic responsibilities, and perhaps go home to her family.

---

37   Once again, we are not here including the other category of call, in respect to the office of the holy ministry.

In other words, it is impossible for the surgeon to be only one segment of herself at any given moment. Her core values accompany her; her morals and ethics are innate; her worldview and fundamental beliefs will continue to define her. For the Christian, nothing defines her as much as her faith. Where there is no faith, there can be no vocation/calling from God. Faith is the created medium that evidences the vertical call and drives the love of horizontal calls.

Vocations require our whole being involved in whatever we do, wherever we go. We don't turn our vocational lights on and off. They are always on.[38] To simplify, that heart surgeon will have to speak to the loved ones after the surgery. How will she communicate? Will it be with the care and compassion of Christ's light, or will it be with something else? How will that surgeon treat her colleagues? How will the surgeon present herself in public as a representative of her field and profession? How will she contribute to the culture in other ways?

The point is that for Christians it is impossible that our vertical call from God making us Christ's light-bearers would *not* impact, affect, and influence our horizontal calls as we serve the people around us. Of course, it will. Of course, it must.[39]

C. S. Lewis wrote, "I believe in Christianity as I believe that the Sun has risen, not only because I see it, but because by it I see everything else."[40] Coming to faith in Jesus Christ by virtue of the vertical call shining His light upon us makes our horizontal calls look brand new. We begin to see the rest of the story in them. We can see their true significance. Through the light of Christ, we can see—as Lewis wrote—*everything else.*

---

38   Recall that vocation is from the Latin *vocare*, which means "to call," and it may be used to refer to our singular vocation as baptized children of God or our many calls through which we serve our neighbors.

39   This, of course, must be tempered as the theology of the cross instead of the theology of glory. We cannot expect the new life to be evident to the world. Nevertheless, our vertical call may impact and empower our horizontal calls in unexpected ways.

40   C. S. Lewis, *The Weight of Glory and Other Addresses* (New York: MacMillan, 1949), 92.

At last, our place in our families can make sense, our position at work takes on a significance not previously realized, and our citizenship in our country becomes important and meaningful. Suddenly, the light of Christ shines on everything we are called to do in the world so that we see how God might work through us at every turn while shining and sharing His light.

Part I will give more attention to our vertical call and horizontal calls. Point blank, we usually underestimate the life-altering significance of our vertical call from God. It quite simply changes us. We enter a new status in life, and we are no longer alone in anything we do. Light pervades. God is calling us to confess what is now true for the baptized. That is, we become certain about **who we are.** Then and only then do we begin to see Christ's light in the most mundane and ordinary horizontal calls. Satan's darkness tries to hide how important your calls are in this world, but when the light of Christ is recognized through them, it changes how we look at everything we do on a day-to-day basis. We are indeed light-bearers, and our horizontal calls take on a value and a sanctity we did not see before. Then, we come to know **what we are to do.**

Part II explains the indispensable connection between our call and calls and **where they take place.** But isn't this obvious? The simple answer would seem to be that they all happen in the world. But this is an inadequate reply. God has arranged the arena of our lives to include what we refer to as *estates* or *orders* or *realms.* The Lord wills that His light shine in all three. Regardless of precise terminology, we are talking about unique contexts in and through which God commands us to live. These three estates are **the family, the church, and the state.** We begin with the family because that is where *we* begin! We continue with the church in the sense of its cultural expressions as congregations in the world. And we conclude by looking at the state in a broad sense that not only includes God-established government but also what light-bearers do in the general culture.

Part III goes into the celebratory elaboration of what Christians— the light of the world—do while shining Christ's light in the family, including through the vocation of singleness.[41] Part IV does the same in respect to the church. I will explain why in this section I've chosen to place our call as friends related to the church estate. Part V will be the broadest in scope as it not only considers our vocation as citizens but also our calls in connection to such categories as education, the arts, and, of course, *just* everyday work, where often the light of Christ shines most brightly.

---

41   The holy cross is included in the "celebratory" because, though it is difficult, it leads to great blessings.

INTRODUCTION DISCUSSION GUIDE

Receiving and Reflecting Christ's Light

UNCOVER INFORMATION

1. What is the "light" received by Christians through Word and Sacraments?

2. How does Jesus refer to Himself in John 8:12?

3. How is light reflected according to Matthew 5:14, 16 in a practical way?

4. How are Christians supposed to live or "walk"?

5. What are the two major kinds of calls?

DISCOVER MEANING

1. Regarding the answer to question 1 above, why is it important to know the answer?

2. According to Christ's own words in John 8:12, what are the benefits given to those who follow Him?

3. Why is the practical expression of Matthew 5:16 so important if we share the saving Gospel?

4. What does Scripture mean by "walk as children of light" (Ephesians 5:8)?

5. What do we mean by "vertical" and "horizontal" calls? What is the difference?

EXPLORE IMPLICATIONS

1. If the Christian *receives* such light, how should the Christian respond?

2. If one *does* follow Christ, why does Matthew 5:14a make sense?

3. If a Christian says, "All we do toward the neighbor is verbalize the Gospel apart from good works," why is this short-sighted?

4. When walking as children of light, how might Christians affect the darkness in the world?

5. How is the vertical call supposed to impact the many horizontal calls?

PART I

Christp the Light of the World Calls Christians

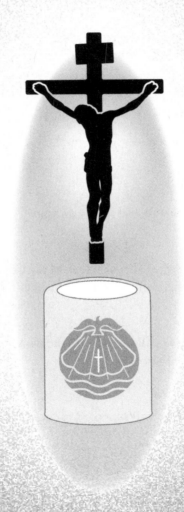

CHAPTER 1

CHRIST'S LIGHT *UPON* US
(THE VERTICAL CALL)

Christ's One-of-a-Kind Call That Changes Everything

The Christian's vertical call is a micro-creation event reminiscent of the macro-event recorded in Genesis 1. Before this call upon the individual, there was nothing but death (Ephesians 2:1). Before this call, darkness reigned. But the moment God called from above, in that very moment, we passed from death to life (John 5:24). Once life did not exist. Then, the call put Christ's light upon us, and from that time forth Christ's new life was imputed to us.[42] The Scripture is true: "Therefore, if anyone is in Christ, he is a new creation" (2 Corinthians 5:17).

God calls us to believe it. Faith holds to what God says. The Lord did what He did when you were baptized into Christ, that "we too might walk in newness of life" (Romans 6:4). This is the work of God requiring nothing—and nothing means *nothing*—from us. We don't coax creation, facilitate it, prepare it, guarantee it, initiate it, help it, nor open it.

The vertical call from God is 100 percent noncontingent on us or anyone or anything else. There were no primordial photons that got together and conspired, "Okay, fellas, when the Christ says, 'Let there be light,' we jump into action to help Him out!" Before His call-command at the cosmic event, not even photons existed. Before His call-command at the conversion event, not even man's accepting will existed. It is for

---

42   This is divine monergism over unbiblical synergism.

us now to believe it, but this, too, is the result of the call, because God's call creates the very faith required to hold on to Jesus.

Now that I've brought out the distinction between the one and only vertical call and the several horizontal calls we have in this life, let me make this perfectly clear: God's Word *by far* emphasizes the vertical call. The number of Scripture references ascribed to either can hardly be compared. The vertical call is all over the New Testament, while the texts relating to horizontal calls are few and far between even while they are vital. The point, however, is that the order and priority is clear. There can be no meaningful consideration of our horizontal calls if we miss the foundation and driving force of the vertical call.

Here are some examples of the vertical call, in which the light of Christ is put upon the Christian and by which God calls the believer to Himself, to belong to Christ,and to be saints (created holy ones), guaranteed of God's glory and assured that they will never fail in their election:

> Acts 2:38–39: And Peter said to them, "Repent and be baptized every one of you in the name of Jesus Christ for the forgiveness of your sins, and you will receive the gift of the Holy Spirit. For the promise is for you and for your children and for all who are far off, everyone whom the Lord our God **calls to Himself."**

> Romans 1:5–6: Through whom we have received grace and apostleship to bring about the obedience of faith for the sake of His name among all the nations, including you who are **called to belong to Jesus Christ.**

> 1 Corinthians 1:2: To the church of God that is in Corinth, to those sanctified in Christ Jesus, **called to be saints** together with all those who in every place call upon the name of our Lord Jesus Christ, both their Lord and ours.

> 2 Thessalonians 2:14: To this He **called you through our gospel,** so that you may obtain the glory of our Lord Jesus Christ.

2 Peter 1:10: Therefore, brothers, be all the more diligent to confirm **your calling and election,** for if you practice these qualities you will never fall.

Why Isn't Christ's Call More Evident?

There are a few important reasons for understanding that if these things are true about God's vertical, light-giving call for us (and, of course, they are true), then why is the light of this call so hard to see? Or, for that matter, why don't we just *feel* it the way we think we ought to? Why is it so hard to know that it is even there?

The first reason is the main reason: Christians are made "to be conformed to the image of His Son [Jesus Christ]" (Romans 8:29).[43] In this way, we look like Jesus in His earthly humility to the rest of the world, and for that matter, those in Christ are equally as unimpressive. *We* can't even see *ourselves* in light. Luther said, "A Christian is even hidden from himself; he does not see his holiness and virtue, but sees in himself nothing but unholiness and vice."[44]

Let's be frank, the sinful flesh is unimpressed by Jesus Christ. But we are not surprised. God hides Himself (Isaiah 45:15). He will not substantiate the world's standards as to what is impressive and praiseworthy. He will not lower Himself to the fickle opinions of what is the great thing one day and the bygone fad the next. God won't play that game, so He makes Himself unimpressive according to the world's standards. Indeed, He hides Himself in this way for good reason, and this was how Jesus typically presented Himself during His earthly ministry: "He was despised and rejected by men, a man of sorrows and acquainted with grief; and as one from whom men hide their faces He was despised, and we esteemed Him not" (Isaiah 53:3). Lessing's commentary is helpful here:

Esau "despised" his birthright (Genesis 25:34), while Goliath (1 Samuel 17:42) and Michal (2 Samuel 6:16) both "despised"

---

43   Here we are reflecting on the theology of the cross.

44   AE 35:411.

David. With the same disgust, "we" first scorned the Davidic Servant. Much like Job's "friends," the speakers in Isaiah 53:1–3 were interpreting the Servant's suffering through a theology of glory, not the theology of the cross. The natural human tendency (the . . . "opinion of the Law" ingrained in the human heart) is to judge according to appearances (cf. 1 Samuel 16:7; 2 Corinthians 5:12).[45]

Luther adds the insight in respect to Isaiah 53:3: "This passage forms the basis for the church's faith that Christ's kingdom is not of this world."[46] But isn't Isaiah 53:3 focused on Christ's Passion?[47] The principle of God hiding Himself and being unimpressive to the world, however, applies to all of Jesus' life on earth during the time of His humiliation.[48] Before His Passion, the Scriptures record the reaction of the people who heard His teaching: "'Is not this the carpenter's son? Is not His mother called Mary? And are not His brothers James and Joseph and Simon and Judas? And are not all His sisters with us? Where then did this man get all these things?' And they took offense at Him" (Matthew 12:55–57a). "Familiarity breeds contempt" was even applicable toward Jesus, the light of the world!

Even when the world *should be* impressed, it won't be unless the Holy Spirit opens a way. Christians should not be surprised that the light of Jesus upon them remains hard to see, much less impressive to those around. Like the Christians in Corinth, we are reminded that as we consider our calling, "not many of [us] were wise according to worldly standards, not many were powerful, not many were of noble

---

45   R. Reed Lessing, *Isaiah 40–55*, Concordia Commentary (St. Louis: Concordia Publishing House, 2011), 614.

46   AE 17:220.

47   The Passion of Christ is a period typically ascribed from Christ's prayer in the Garden of Gethsemane up through His holy crucifixion.

48   The state of Christ's humiliation begins after the miracle of the incarnation during His time in Mary's womb all the way through His death and burial. The descent into hell is *not* included in Christ's humiliation. Though it should be said that even in instances of Christ revealing His glory, the sin problem runs so deep that doubt and rejection may persist. Abraham told the rich man in Hades, "If they do not hear Moses and the Prophets, neither will they be convinced if someone should rise from the dead" (Luke 16:31).

birth" (1 Corinthians 1:26). From the world's perspective, our present status might not seem much of an improvement over our prior one.

While St. Matthew would serve in the office of apostle, which is an example of a horizontal call, Matthew 9 describes St. Matthew becoming a disciple. In Matthew 9:9, Jesus was calling St. Matthew to believe.[49] Jesus cast His faith-giving light upon Matthew through His Word, through His call. This is yet another example of the vertical call. *Call* here is not simply to be named, or even furthermore, summoned, but to call into existence—once again, like a micro-cosmic creation event.

It is, however, how Jesus elaborates upon this call a little further into Matthew 9 that helps us see the humble circumstances surrounding such a magnificent call. St. Matthew records the words of Christ: "For I came not to call the righteous, but sinners" (Matthew 9:13b).

Sinners in this case and in the eyes of the world are anything but impressive. They are those who think too highly of themselves. From the perspective of the general public, who would ever be impressed with one known as a *sinner*? And yet it is sinners whom the Lord teaches clearly that He calls. He desires (and He does!) to put His light upon obvious sinners, those who are weak, who struggle, and who are generally totally unimpressive to the rest of the world. This is God's way.

The second reason that it is hard to see or perceive God's light-giving call is on account of the sinful nature. We are—in fact, all people are—on account of the sinful nature, fantastic skeptics. We just don't believe in the good. It is far easier to criticize even ourselves than to accept God's grace that amounts to the greatest gifts to us poor sinners. We just doubt that God could be so loving and merciful toward us. According to the flesh, we can't believe it.

One of the most important examples of horizontal calls in my life are those father-confessors and true pastors who have served me over the years. I am an advocate of every pastor acquiring a pastor and recommend that every pastor look into this gift for themselves.[50]

---

49   Jeffrey A. Gibbs, *Matthew 1:1–11:1*, Concordia Commentary (St. Louis: Concordia Publishing House, 2006), 465.

50   *Confession and Absolution: A Report of the Commission on Theology and Church Relations* (St. Louis: The Lutheran Church—Missouri Synod, 2018).

The first one I saw regularly while serving in southern California was the Rev. Dr. Timothy Seals. Earlier in my ministry, the Lord had shown His light through Pastor Seals upon me in a profound way.

During one of my confessions before Pastor Seals, I opened up about my struggle with sin in such a way that I doubted the grace of God.[51] Pastor Seals did not hesitate to admonish me. While my confession *sounded* contrite, it was in truth an expression of exceeding pride: I was treating my sin as being greater than God's grace in Christ. I was being insistent that the quality of my sin was too much even for Jesus, the light of the world. I will never forget Pastor Seal's admonition. It was exactly what I needed to hear and learn.

Unfortunately, many of us make this move and keep God's light at arm's length because we like to insist that we are just too bad for the light of God. When we do this, not only do we grossly underestimate God's amazing grace, but we feed our own stubbornness and ego as we try to convince ourselves that we are stronger than God, that what we say trumps what God says. When Christ's light comes, however, it comes upon even the worst of sinners. The Holy Spirit inspired St. Paul to write these words:

> Though formerly I was a blasphemer, persecutor, and insolent opponent. But I received mercy because I had acted ignorantly in unbelief, and the grace of our Lord overflowed for me with the faith and love that are in Christ Jesus. The saying is trustworthy and deserving of full acceptance, that Christ Jesus came into the world to save sinners, of whom I am the foremost. But I received mercy for this reason, that in me, as the foremost, Jesus Christ might display His perfect patience as an example to those who were to believe in Him for eternal life.[52]

When the devil, the world, and even our own sinful nature accuse us and try to convince us that we are too far gone for the light of Christ,

---

51   The pastor is bound to never divulge what is confessed to him. I was not the confessor here but the penitent.

52   1 Timothy 1:13–16.

let us remind them all that they lie to us and that Jesus is just who He says He is: the friend of sinners (Matthew 11:19).

The third reason we try to convince ourselves that Christ's light upon us cannot be seen is because the Lord is intentionally teaching us to walk by faith and not by sight (2 Corinthians 5:7). This takes us back to the theology of the cross. Just as faith must see Jesus as truly God though He suffers and die, just as faith must see in the simple and paltry bread and wine the body and blood of the almighty Savior, it is also the case that faith must see the sinner on earth who nevertheless has faith in Jesus, a saint on earth who is holy in the sight of God. Faith sees that we really are what God says we are. Therefore, the Christian faith considers the ear—when opened by the Holy Spirit to hear with created faith—to be more important than the eye. Our eyes easily deceive us, so instead we trust more in what we hear from God's Word as children of light. Luther says this:

> [God] simply wants the forgiveness of sins, which alone grants joy, to come only through the Word or only through hearing. For if you tortured yourself to death, if you shed your blood, if with ready heart you underwent and bore everything that is humanly possible—all this would not help you. Only hearing brings joy. This is the only way for the heart to find peace before God.[53]

To put it mildly, we struggle with this. We would rather see. You know the saying "Seeing is believing." The saying, however, is potentially disastrous. Our eyes deceive us all the time, especially when it comes to the light of Christ. Therefore, we need the Word of Christ. God revealed to the psalmist: "Your word is a lamp to my feet and a light to my path" (Psalm 119:105). We need the light of God's Word over and above what we see with our eyes or conclude with our sinful reason. Sinful reason tries to bypass the hearing of the Word, and it tries to run away from God's light. Even as we use our reason to observe ourselves, we easily mislead ourselves.

---

53   AE 12:368.

After my first call in southern California, I commenced my second call in the area of Houston, Texas. There, I was blessed again with another father-confessor. This time Rev. Dr. Scott Murray who—like my first father-confessor—was faithful in his holy vocation as pastor. That is, through him the light of Christ streamed upon me.

For private confession and absolution, we would sometimes go into his sanctuary. He would kneel beside me and hear my confession. On this occasion, I was surprised that he interrupted my confession in front of God and me. What was he doing? I had just confessed my inconsistency in praying for the people of my parish since every pastor is called also to pray for his flock. But again, Pastor Murray butted in. He stopped me in my tracks before I could finish and asked, "But why aren't you praying for them consistently?" I was flabbergasted if not a little annoyed by his unexpected intrusion. I thought about his question and said in so many words, "Well, sometimes my heart isn't where it should be." He looked at me in utter bewilderment as he asked, "What does your heart have to do with anything?"

He went on to admonish me and instruct me in the most kind and loving tone. Nevertheless, he was bold and "in my face" as a true spiritual father. He explained, "Al, you don't pray because you feel like praying, but because God has commanded you to pray and because God has promised you His blessing when you do. It matters not how you feel. Pray because God commands you and because God has promised to bless you." He was, of course, elaborating right out of Luther's Large Catechism.[54]

The Vertical Call Is *Continuous,* and the Light of Christ Is *Always* upon Us

In our sacred biblical theology, creation has as its corollary preservation. God's power through His call that created the heavens and the earth continues also to *preserve* the heavens and the earth. It is always in play. The same is true regarding Christians called to be children of light. We should not think of the vertical call—while being utterly unique

---

54   Large Catechism III, The Lord's Prayer.

and one—as something past. It is a call that keeps us in the status of children of light past, present, and future; it is an enduring call.

The light of Christ through the Word and Sacraments shines on us not as a one-time zap but as perpetual radiation. Not only is it responsible for making us new, but it is completely responsible for keeping us new. For example, this vertical call and light keeps us in faith that is *constantly* repenting. Jesus said, "Just so, I tell you, there will be more joy in heaven over one sinner who repents than over ninety-nine righteous persons who need no repentance" (Luke 15:7). The original Greek verb is a "present participle [which] is durative and expresses the fact that repentance goes on and on," as Lenski taught and then pointed out, "Luther was right when in the first of his famous ninety-five theses he declared that our entire life must be continuous repentance."[55]

Psalm 27:1 depicts the Lord our light and stronghold: "The LORD is my light and my salvation, whom shall I fear? The LORD is the stronghold of my life; of whom shall I be afraid?" We know that we may *continually* take refuge in Him.[56] His light never departs from us. Psalm 34:5 tells us: "Those who look to Him are radiant, and their faces shall never be ashamed." This looking upon the Lord is in the perfect tense.[57] There is a never a time we *can't* look to Him and be radiant. Psalm 36:9: "For with You is the fountain of life; in Your light do we see light." This is the light of the "fullness of salvation."[58] When is this not true for those in Christ? Psalm 80:3, which includes the words "let Your face shine," is reminiscent of the Aaronic blessing in Numbers 6:25: "The LORD make His face to shine upon you and be gracious to you." H. C. Leupold concludes, "So potent is God's good pleasure that, as soon as it becomes operative, deliverance sets in."[59] When does it become operative in the child of God? The moment he or she received the vertical call and was made new through water and the Word past tense *and* through the life constantly receiving Word and Sacrament present and future tense.

---

55   R. C. H. Lenski, *The Interpretation of St. Luke's Gospel* (Minneapolis: Augsburg, 1946), 801.

56   H. C. Leupold, *Exposition of Psalms* (Grand Rapids, MI: Baker Book House, 1959), 236.

57   Leupold, *Exposition of Psalms*, 280.

58   Leupold, *Exposition of Psalms*, 296.

59   Leupold, *Exposition of Psalms*, 581.

Christ's Light upon Those in Him Is Irrevocable

God's Word reveals, "Jesus Christ is the same yesterday and today and forever" (Hebrews 13:8). This Scripture is one among others establishing the article of faith, meaning that our light does not change.[60] This is also clear in the Old Testament. God spoke through the prophet: "For I the LORD do not change, therefore you, O children of Jacob, are not consumed" (Malachi 3:6).

The author of Hebrews was encouraging the congregation to emulate their past leaders, but this was no glorification of persons but rather a reminder of what remains constant among the faithful. John W. Kleinig puts the Word in context: "These leaders may have now left the world, but what they believed still remains, because 'Jesus Christ is the Same One—yesterday, today and forever.'"[61] And Theo Laetsch points out that Malachi's revelation of God's unchanging nature is also true of His grace for sinners.

> [God's] unalterable holiness and justice does not cancel or even interfere with His unchanging grace and mercy . . . [this is] the God of unchanging grace. His grace makes it possible that their sorrow will become godly sorrow working repentance unto salvation.[62]

So, Holy Scripture makes it plain that both the person of Christ and the grace of Christ do not change. What might this suggest regarding His call to His people? St. Paul provides a lucid answer: "For the gifts and the calling of God are irrevocable" (Romans 11:29). His vertical call of light upon the Christian cannot be taken back. God will not take it back, and it is this call that provides a way for us to come back to Christ if we ever stray as sheep sometimes do.

---

60   The article of faith called the immutability of God.

61   John W. Kleinig, *Hebrews*, Concordia Commentary (St. Louis: Concordia Publishing House, 2017), 699–700.

62   Theo Laetsch, *Commentary on the Minor Prophets* (St. Louis: Concordia Publishing House, 1956), 537.

In the context of Romans 11, the call (in time), even to the Israelites who rejected the Lord, remained intact. But the overall principle is maintained, as Michael P. Middendorf reminds us that *all people* are called to faith by the Gospel process described in Romans 10:16–17.[63] And the Lord will not change His mind: His call for the salvation even for the worst of sinners *will not be revoked.*

It is for us now—by the power of the Holy Spirit—to believe it. If our call in Christ is never revoked, and if the light of Christ never ceases to shine upon us, then we can have great confidence about our new lives in Christ. Some might even see us as being prodigal with God's light, lavishly reflecting it wherever we go.[64] Saving faith not only holds to this vertical call but rejoices in it. It is our irrevocable call. May we never reject it, but furthermore, may we never be shy about it either. This call is designed to empower us to *live for God by* loving and serving our neighbors through our horizontal calls, and it is a call that we should be 100 percent confident about.

Christ's Light Should Make Christians Confident

Traci and I have been blessed with grandchildren. One of them, the one I call *Mr. Man* (as well as the Spanish equivalent of the title), is just a year and some months old. He already has a few horizontal calls under his belt. One of them, of course, is that he is my grandson, which has generated another horizontal call for me as his grandfather. In this case, allow me to use my relationship with Mr. Man as an analogy for God's vertical call to the Christian and the resultant confidence every Christian should have about their call from God.

Mr. Man was called into our family. His middle name is the middle name I gave to his dad, my son, Mr. Man's father. Of course, he also took my surname. He *received my name, "Espinosa," and now he reflects my entire family and, yes, me too, his grandpa*. To make matters more

---

63   Michael P. Middendorf, *Romans 9–16*, Concordia Commentary (St. Louis: Concordia Publishing House, 2016), 1173.

64   Timothy Keller wrote a great book entitled *The Prodigal God: Recovering the Heart of the Christian Faith* (New York: Dutton, 2008) in which he presents the main point of the parable of the prodigal son: the overflowing and lavish grace of God that many viewed as wasteful toward the undeserving son.

interesting, this little guy looks like me too, at least when he's running around getting into things with that grin on his face and look in his eye.

It's the running around part, however, that should be highlighted. When Traci and I moved back to California from Texas, we brought several of our children with us. We needed space, and the Lord provided a rather roomy residence. Since that time, however, Traci and I have become empty nesters. We are starting to enjoy the extra space available to us, including the study upstairs I've always dreamed about.

Traci babysits Mr. Man, so he is often over to the house during the day. In fact, as far as he is concerned, he has *two* homes. When he is at ours, he runs around like he owns the place and, in his mind, he is probably convinced that he does. Traci and I just smile. We are happy that he gets the significance of his call. He is confident, secure, and joyful in our home. He exudes the significance of his call. He is not ashamed of it. He celebrates it, and it comes out in the way he smiles at us.

But his confidence goes beyond his second home, as it is frequently expressed toward me. He is a big talker at such an early age, so he will often rampage into my space, saying, "Grandpa!" When I look at him, he has this electric smile shining back at me. He is utterly comfortable and confident in my arms and does not hesitate to ask me for whatever is on his mind. This contact fuels him up with even more confidence about who and what he is. This back and forth between reception and reflection is enabling him to go out into the world with confidence.

It is our vertical call from God that energizes our other calls in the world. Christ's light that shines through us will be in direct proportion to the light of Christ that shines upon us. If we run from His vertical light, then we should never be surprised if His horizontal light through us is less than bright. But when we relish this strong, beyond sight, continuous, and irrevocable call, then watch out: we will know the key to Christ shining through us in our daily vocations. We will understand that our mission in our lives on earth is to shine, to love, and to serve, to reflect Jesus Christ in whatever we are doing in our horizontal calls.

Mr. Man still has his issues. He cries like other toddlers. He gets boo boos sometimes when he falls, he gets tired and gets grouchy, he gets his feelings hurt by other children, and he gets upset when he doesn't want to leave grandma and grandpa. He still struggles through life, but he knows his family and his voice. He knows with a confidence what makes him strong.

Christ's Call Always Leads to Good

The faithful pastor who catechized and confirmed me, the late Rev. John A. Miller III, chose to give me Romans 8:28 as my confirmation verse. Like many Christians, I've come to love this verse in God's Word. It has been a steady help and comfort to me.

St. Paul wrote by inspiration of the Holy Spirit: "And we know that for those who love God all things work together for good, for those who are called according to His purpose" (Romans 8:28). This one verse the Lord has used to guide me through many storms in my life. I have been immensely consoled over the years that God in this Scripture is not saying that *all things* are good. No, God's Word makes clear that there are many things that are not. The significance of the verse, however, is that God *works good even through those things that are not good*, and as I've learned, sometimes especially so.

And the Lord does this always for a reason even though frequently—if not always—in the middle of the storm we have no idea as to why what is happening is happening. Often, we cannot see *anything* good coming out of our messes. When we feel this way, it is easy to be tempted in all directions and hypothesize:

1. God is punishing me.

2. God has abandoned me.

3. God is unfair or unjust.

These comprise just the short list of our pessimistic theories. But the Lord always has His reasons. He does not call us to understand. Rather, He calls us to trust Him. When I was growing up, I would frequently ask my mother of sacred memory, "But why?" Her response was predictable and exquisitely consistent: "Because I said so." I yearned for more. I wanted to understand. Since I knew I had experienced so much frustration in this typical back-and-forth growing up, I vowed to myself that I would be a different kind of parent. "When my children ask why, I will talk to them, teaching them as a patient, loving, and sage parent." I had it all mapped out.

Then my time came as a father with many opportunities with many children. I had quite the variety of responses to my willingness to talk, and talk, and talk. For instance, you probably have heard it enough on TV police dramas that the Miranda rights script is familiar by now. It includes, "Anything you say can and will be used against you in a court of law." Though the situation in the family may not be quite as serious as all that, still, because my words—even with tireless elaboration—were still misunderstood or later taken out of context, I never knew what would come back to bite me. At the end of the day, I realized that what my mother was teaching me was the most important lesson and it applies to our faith: just do what God says. The most important thing He says to us is "Believe! Trust! Have faith!"

When we ask, "Why?" watch out, because we can convince ourselves that we can know the mind of God, that we understand the big picture and can smooth over all the complexities. We could not be further from the truth.

God's Word provides many reasons as to why Christians suffer, but in the Book of Job there is no reason given for Job's extreme plight.[65] I know someone who I think has used this one fact to evidently turn from the faith. "How could God permit such suffering upon a faithful child?" We can't concoct a rational explanation, so it must be that God

---

65   While the Book of Job never provides a stated reason for Job's suffering, there are many revealed reasons in Scripture as to why a Christian might suffer besides the universal reasons of sin's impact upon the world and the consequences of actual sin. Some of the additional reasons include being persecuted for righteousness' sake (Matthew 5:10), taking up the cross to follow Christ (Matthew 16:24), the tribulations in the world affecting Christians in particular (John 16:33), suffering dishonor for the name of Jesus (Acts 5:41), martyrdom (Acts 7:58–60), the distress of the inner battle (Romans 7:24), suffering with Christ in order to be glorified with Him (Romans 8:17), affliction that permits the experience of comfort in order to comfort those who enter the same affliction (2 Corinthians 1:4), crucifying the flesh (Galatians 5:24), bearing others' burdens in love (Galatians 6:2), wrestling against spiritual forces of evil (Ephesians 6:12), suffering loss to gain Christ (Philippians 3:8), filling up what is lacking in Christ's afflictions (Colossians 1:24), the consequences of desiring to live a godly life in Christ (2 Timothy 3:12), and enduring the discipline of the Lord (Hebrews 12:5–6). All these are used by God to bless our faith in Christ so that we might receive the crown of eternal life, at which time we will realize more than ever His working good through all things.

is guilty, God is wrong. But this is exactly where *we* would be wrong. The Lord is calling us to trust His call and to witness His light, which accomplishes good through anything we go through, even when what we go through is not good. When faith holds that Christ's light will never be taken from us, we can be strong even or especially when we are weak (2 Corinthians 12:10). That is, when we feel most weak, we are most apt to fall into the arms of our strong Savior, Jesus. What does such a faith look like?

One of the best examples of such faith is seen in the Syrophoenician woman in Mark 7. In Matthew's parallel, Jesus praised her at the end of their encounter: "O woman, great is your faith! Be it done for you as you desire" (Matthew 15:28). Luther was magnificent in his description of her faith:

> She runs after Him into the house—as Mark [7:24–25] writes—perseveres, falls down before Him, and says, "Lord, help me!" [Matt. 15:25]. There she gets the final deathblow, when He says directly to her (as the words read) that she is a dog and unworthy to share the children's bread [Matt. 15:26]. What will she say to this? He simply asserts that she is one of the damned and lost, who is not to be numbered among the elect. That is an answer that can never be contested, one that no one can get past. Yet she does not cease, but concedes His judgment and that she is a dog. She desires also no more than a dog, namely, to "eat the crumbs that fall from their masters' table" [Matt. 15:27]. Is not that a masterpiece? She clutches at Christ's own words. He compares her to a dog; she grants that and asks nothing more than that He would let her be a dog, as He Himself had judged her to be. Where could He go? He is captured. We let a dog have the crumbs under the table; that is its right. Therefore, He now completely opens His heart to her and yields to her will, so that she is now not a dog, but a child of Israel [Matt. 15:28].[66]

---

66   AE 76:380. Brackets in original.

The split second we feel unworthy like a dog, that is when we should remember just how brightly the light of Christ shines upon us. This call from above, our singular and yet ever-streaming vertical call makes us who are so low, so doubtful, so weak, so up and down, so not-where-we-wish-we-were in life, the perfect candidates for Jesus, who came for sinners. His call to us has changed everything in our lives. He won't take it back, and it provides every reason for us to be confident about who we are as children of light.

Yes, Jesus is the light of the world (John 8:12), and He—the almighty Lord—says to all His disciples: "You are the light of the world" (Matthew 5:14). Christ's light has come upon us and when we believe in and confess His name, we are to anticipate His light shining through us. It might not be in the way we expect or in the way others might like it to, but it will shine in the way God wants it to. Indeed, the vertical call is the greatest call, the most vital vocation. It's time now to understand what is going on within horizontal calls.

CHAPTER 1 DISCUSSION GUIDE

Christ's Light *upon* Us
(The Vertical Call)

UNCOVER INFORMATION

1. What happened the moment we received God's vertical call?

2. The vertical call is contingent on whom alone?

3. Is the vertical call in the life of the Christian self-evident or easily seen?

4. Why do we say that the vertical call is continuous and not just a one-time thing?

5. How long is God's vertical call for the Christian good for?

DISCOVER MEANING

1. The vertical call might be referred to as a micro-_____ event.

2. What does the Christian "do" to receive the vertical call?

3. What are the three main reasons why the vertical call is hard to see?

4. Why does the Christian need to be repenting constantly?

5. What do we mean by "God's call is irrevocable"?

EXPLORE IMPLICATIONS

1. When Christians receive this call from God, they pass from what to what?

2. According to the five Scriptures listed in this chapter, what can we say about the vertical call?

3. What is required of the Christian to hold that the vertical call is real and true for him or her?

4. The Word of God for us is applied to our call, past, present, and future. Why does the Christian need this?

5. How should the fact that God's call is irrevocable affect the Christian?

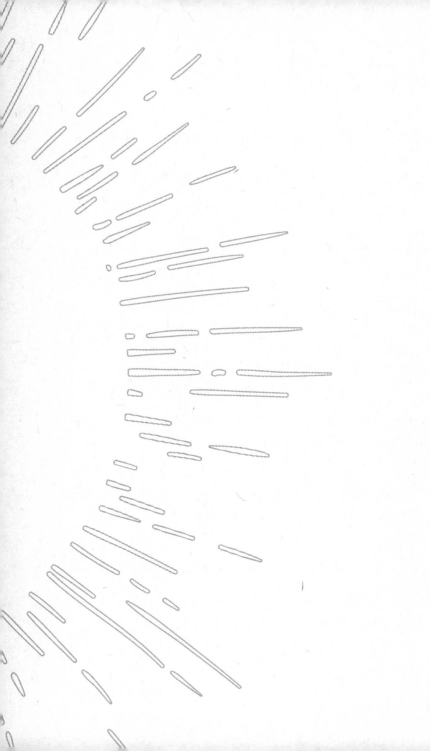

CHAPTER 2

CHRIST'S LIGHT *THROUGH* US
(THE HORIZONTAL CALLS UNDERSTOOD)

Christ Shining through His Masks

Our horizontal callings can never be reduced to our jobs, but our employment *is included* among our callings, and when we realize this, our jobs will never be looked at in the same way. On two different occasions, I met two unique men who drove taxis for a living.[67] On both occasions, I was richly blessed, as the Lord helped me considerably through them.

The first was in San Francisco. Traci and I have learned the importance of rest, especially as I serve in pastoral ministry, and she supports me in ways hard to understand by anyone who is not a pastor's wife. We get away to rejuvenate and to make taking care of our marriage a priority.

As we walked through the lobby of our downtown hotel, we found the concierge. Our question was important, because we had a serious craving for pizza, but the pizza had to be gluten-free. The concierge demonstrated his exceptional knowledge of the city and knew exactly where to send us. He promised we would love it and gave us directions.

It was such a gorgeous day that Traci and I decided to walk. It was a long walk, about five miles, but we loved it. It was an adventure and a lot of fun to walk through the city side by side. When we found the pizza place just across from Oracle Park, where the Giants play, we were thrilled. The restaurant looked like a little Italy. Our host was gracious,

---

67   For anyone too young to know what a taxi is, just think Uber or Lyft.

welcoming us as she put the menus in front of us. Her smile, however, quickly fell when I told her how excited we were to find a place with gluten-free pizza. With a look of gloom she answered, "Sir, I'm so sorry, but we only offer gluten-free at our *other* location!" We couldn't believe what we were hearing.

It was starting to get late, but with a newfound determination, I checked my watch. Traci could read my mind. "Oh honey, it's okay, I can get a salad." She didn't understand. Such an egregious compromise wasn't happening. I jumped out of my chair and ran outside, Traci doing her best to tail me. Just as the Giants' game had let out, with pandemonium in the streets, I was able to flag a taxi while running to it. I waved my arms at Traci to hurry, and we managed to jump in ahead of about ten others lined up for the same cab. We were suddenly in one of those movie scenes: after giving him the address and closing time, there I was asking him to *step on it.*

As for this taxi driver, as far as I am concerned, he must have been sent from heaven. When I said, "Step on it," *he did.*

Recall, we were in San Francisco. Our ride to this other restaurant was like a roller coaster. There were at least a couple times that I felt tires off the ground. We laughed, probably to chase away fright. We were there in record time. After thanking the driver profusely, the host was equally as accommodating to let us in just minutes before closing, and there we were ordering gluten-free pizza and a bottle of wine.

How did this happen? In retrospect, it felt like something approaching chariots of fire, but in this instance, it was a taxi driver. God worked through this man not only to help us reach food to sustain our bodies but also to grant Traci and me one of our most cherished memories symbolizing our love. God blessed us through this taxi driver.

Strictly speaking, horizontal calls combine the call from God to the faith of the one receiving the call while confessing the Caller and then going forth understanding what vocation does in reflecting Christ. Gustaf Wingren summarized this important distinction: "All have station (*Stand*) and office; but *Beruf* [call] is the Christian's earthly or spiritual work."[68] But what if the one serving does not have this faith? Then God still works through them as they carry out their God-appointed stations even if it is without faith. Nevertheless, God is still working either way.

Because the Lord works through very humble people, we refer to these people as the *masks* of God. God is there, but we see the person. It is as if God were wearing a mask as He serves through people. Luther gives further insight:

> God could easily give you grain and fruit without your plowing and planting. . . . He could give children without using men and women. But He does not want to do this. Instead, He joins man and woman so that it appears to be the work of man and woman, and yet He does it under the cover of such masks. We have the saying: "God gives every good thing, but not just by waving a wand." God gives all good gifts; but you must lend a hand and take the bull by the horns; that is, you must work and thus give God good cause and a mask.[69]

Let me get to that other taxi driver. Years after San Francisco, I had the privilege to serve my eldest son and his wife by driving a U-Haul from their university in New Haven, Connecticut, to their new apartment in St. Louis, Missouri, where he was starting seminary and she a graduate program in biomedical engineering. It was quite the enterprise, and we were ecstatic to finally make it to St. Louis. We couldn't immediately access their apartment, and so we stayed in a hotel upon arrival. Though exhausted from the trip, I knew my son and daughter-in-law would love to see St. Louis, their new home.

I found a taxi, and we had no idea what the ride would turn into. The driver was someone who confessed faith in God, and it opened the door for me to talk about the Gospel in explicit detail. He rejoiced to

---

68   Gustaf Wingren, *Luther on Vocation* (Eugene, OR: Wipf and Stock, 1957), 2. *Stand* is German for "standing" or "office"; *Beruf* is German for "call" or "vocation," through which the Christian serves in his or her office through faith in God and love for the neighbor.

69   AE 14:114–15.

hear it, and before we knew it, we all felt like an old friend was driving us around. He took us to our restaurant by the Arch for dinner, and he came back to get us, but when he did, he morphed into a tour guide (as he was now off the clock) and took us on a magnificent romp through the city on a gorgeous night. It felt as though the Lord was greeting my son and his wife in His name. This taxi driver was God's sign to them that He was going to bless their time in St. Louis.

Both taxi drivers appeared to be God masks, that is, both were agents of God reflecting God's service and help. God worked through them to bless us. No, we could not see the Lord in His glory as radiant created light, but there He was nevertheless, wearing a mask as two different cab drivers, one in San Francisco and the other in St. Louis.

The Scripture on Horizontal Calls

While there are many Scriptures that acknowledge horizontal calls in God's Word, pointing to soldiers, priests, governors, husbands, wives, apostles, and artisans, there is only one section in God's Word that appears to establish horizontal calls. Gary D. Badcock elaborates:

> There is no suggestion that a biblical "calling" has reference to any secular mode of life or to any form of employment. There is, in fact, only one possible exception to this in the whole of the New Testament, found in 1 Corinthians 7:17–24.[70]

Here is that Scripture:

> Only let each person lead the life that the Lord has assigned to him, and to which God has called him. This is my rule in all the churches. Was anyone at the time of his call already circumcised? Let him not seek to remove the marks of circumcision. Was anyone at the time of his call uncircumcised? Let him not seek circumcision. For neither circumcision counts for anything nor uncircumcision, but keeping the commandments of God. Each one should remain in the condition in

---

70   Gary D. Badcock, *The Way of Life* (Grand Rapids, MI: William B. Eerdmans, 1998), 6.

which he was called. Were you a bondservant when called? Do not be concerned about it. (But if you can gain your freedom, avail yourself of the opportunity.) For he who was called in the Lord as a bondservant is a freedman of the Lord. Likewise, he who was free when called is a bondservant of Christ. You were bought with a price; do not become bondservants of men. So, brothers, in whatever condition each was called, there let him remain with God.

While it seems ludicrous to say that God *needs* anything, Luther made a point that in accord with God's will and plan for us, it indeed appears *as if* God permits Himself to have need: "For he has need of many and various offices and stations and therefore he bestows many different kinds of gifts, so contriving things that one always needs the other and none can do without the other."[71] Our horizontal calls, however, not only put us in the position to be there for others, but they inherently put us into the hands of Christ for our sanctification. "For he appoints many different offices, and Christ, the Son of God who sits at the right hand of the Father, bestows many gifts, in order that he may test us and see whether we fear him and are willing to serve him therein and thus humble ourselves."[72]

Just as our justification is completely by Christ, so is our sanctification, our new lives in Christ. In holy vocation through these horizontal calls, we are the extensions of Christ Himself. God is acting through us and putting upon Himself a mask: they look like you and me. Pause here for a moment and soak this in. Is there anything in this world more worthy of honor than to be God's direct emissary?

But the world does not see nor believe in such honor. Dominated by the flesh, we think our lives as nothing but our own. The world, our sinful nature, and the devil do not want us to consider what we do as calls from God. We treat the question "What will I do with my life?"

---

71   AE 51:351–52.
72   AE 51:352.

as devoid of any concept of duty from God, which "is totally foreign to modern culture."[73]

We forget that God's Word says, "You are not your own, for you were bought with a price" (1 Corinthians 6:19–20). The world, however, cannot run from the fact that what we devote our lives to—the very stations we serve in—are the ethical agent themselves through which God is active on earth.[74] If we lack faith to see this and to celebrate it, God will still work through us, but we will lose out on the incredible insight of just how important our calls are. We will also fail to give proper thanks and glory to God for them.

So, how should the Christian answer the question "What will I do with my life?" Properly speaking it "can be answered for the Christian only in terms of love, for love is the way of Christ Himself, and the way of the God who sent Him into the world."[75]

Our Calls Are Crosses

To be blunt, crosses are symbols of death. In and of themselves, there is nothing pleasant about them. They represent suffering, and oftentimes "suffering" is an understatement in describing what they can cause. In general, however, when applied to the Christian who is to "take up his cross" (Matthew 16:24), they describe some part of the Christian person being put to death so that the Christian might do what he ought to do.

On a small scale, and yet what turned out to be a poignant example to me of picking up the cross in holy vocation, I had a front-row seat to observe two of my grandchildren, Natalie, who was at the time three, and Mr. Man (yes, him again), who was barely one, if that.

Since my wife babysits, I will prepare breakfast oatmeal for the crew on a regular basis. I don't mess around with the oatmeal, as I present it complete with bananas, blueberries, a dash of brown sugar, and a slight pouring of two-percent milk. As we have Fiestaware in the kitchen, I also make sure that each grandchild is provided his or her favorite color bowl.

---

73   Badcock, *The Way of Life*, 44.

74   Wingren, *Luther on Vocation*, 6.

75   Badcock, *The Way of Life*, 112.

Now while at times I will serve up to five or so grandchildren at once, within the crowd both Natalie and Mr. Man are ferocious oatmeal gobblers. They *love* their oatmeal more so than any of the other grandchildren.

One morning, Mr. Man consumed his oatmeal in record time and started crying for more while Traci held him on her lap. It was what I witnessed next that made me believe that there is hope for the future. Natalie, while seemingly preoccupied with her oatmeal as well as one of her favorite cartoons, tore herself away from both to see what was wrong with Mr. Man. I saw her look at him, then look at her oatmeal. She got up, walked over to him, handed her bowl to grandma, and watched as a portion of her remaining oatmeal was transferred to Mr. Man's bowl.

As this transfer was happening, Natalie had teared up. She was holding back her own tears because she was losing some of her precious oatmeal, and yet she wanted to do it because she loves her little brother so much. This was a glimpse of a Christian sister loving her brother in holy vocation. God was serving up more oatmeal for Mr. Man through his loving sister Natalie.

"Vocation, in short, is a cross."[76] And this "cross is not chosen by us; it is laid upon us by God, i.e., the cross comes to us uninvoked in our vocation."[77] Indeed, what I saw in my little granddaughter Natalie was her being compelled and led. She really didn't *want* to do what she was doing, though the Lord made His will hers as she did it. This is to say that in our vertical call, which shines Christ's light, our old man doesn't want to serve the neighbor in love, but our new man wouldn't have it any other way.

In this way, we take on a cross that keeps killing the sinful, self-serving self so that we might live for others. Holy vocation means that we no longer live for ourselves but for others. We truly become reflections of the life of Christ, who "came not to be served but to serve, and to give His life as a ransom for many" (Matthew 20:28).

---

76   Badcock, *The Way of Life*, 39.

77   Wingren, *Luther on Vocation*, 53.

So Badcock elaborates: "The devoted father 'lives,' in a very real sense, for his family; the skilled craftsman derives satisfaction in a job well done—'beautiful and useful' is his ruling principle; the ward sister, underpaid and overworked, fulfills a moral duty in nursing the sick."[78] In this proper way of viewing our lives, our anxious wonderings about whether we are doing what God willed for us are answered. "All the external, daily events which form the course of a man's life are guided by God and proceed from His will."[79]

Our Calls Are Intended to Bless and Free Us

God has given our horizontal calls to us, permitting us to represent Him to the world for the sake of our neighbors and filling our lives with meaning and purpose. What we receive in them is a great gift seen only with eyes of faith. Badcock cuts to the chase here:

> In the synoptic Gospels, all discipleship is presented as the result of Jesus' personal calling; there is no instance of anyone volunteering successfully to become a disciple. It seems, rather, that Jesus' summons has a literally miraculous effect on those called.[80]

Without our even trying, Christ's "miraculous effect" comes upon us and through us. Think about this blessing: "Man is thereby put into right relation both to earth (love) and to heaven (faith). God's complete work is set in motion."[81] What a treasure we've been given, and in it we are set free to live as God desires we would: "This freedom in His possession of the created things man uses in the course, the station, which the Creator gives him, and in which God is present with him, constantly adding to life on earth things that are fresh and new."[82]

---

78   Badcock, *The Way of Life*, 71.

79   Wingren, *Luther on Vocation*, 71.

80   Badcock, *The Way of Life*, 5.

81   Wingren, *Luther on Vocation*, 33.

82   Wingren, *Luther on Vocation*, 219.

This brings a vitality to what we do as we see the marvelous purpose of horizontal calls, which shed the light of Christ upon the world. For such service, we are to understand that God makes the person new when we approach our calls in faith. Luther recounts when the prophet Samuel spoke to King Saul:

> "You will be turned into another man; and whatever your hand finds to do, that you do" [1 Samuel 10:6–7]. He has not prescribed any law for him; but whatever matter presents itself, that he should take on, on that he should work. . . . Always stick to that which lies at hand and belongs to your calling. If you are a preacher or minister of the Word of God, stay with the reading of Scripture and the office of preaching; do not get caught up into something else until the Lord Himself catches you up. For whatever the Lord has not said or commanded will be worthless.[83]

Wingren reminds us that without this insight of our calls as blessings, then our labor is seen *only* as a cross. How often have we been overcome by the flesh to just focus on the time, counting the minutes to stop working? But the "new man, whose heart rejoices in his neighbor, has freedom 'to do or to leave undone,' a freedom which the old man only claims to have."[84] That is the Christian born from above with the light of Christ shining in and through her, who will recognize that what God has called her to do gives her freedom to be what God has made her to be. And—at the same time—Christians have freedom to recognize what they are *not* called to do and with peace walk away from these things. This is freedom for the conscience and for life itself.

When the light of Christ shines upon us and then through us, life is where it ought to be. Life is calibrated in a such a way as to enable us to experience a "sweet spot," or a place where our ability to do what God calls us to do is done naturally in accord with the gifts and abilities

---

83   AE 15:151.

84   Wingren, *Luther on Vocation*, 231.

granted us. The work may be difficult, but we can also easily feel as though we are designed to do it.

To live in this design, however heavy the cross might be, is freedom from the slavery of sin to live for self. It is freedom to enjoy the God-provided skill to do what God wants us to do. Any other work is forced and represents a slavery to ambition that is anything but freedom, even when a person claims to be doing whatever they want to do.

The New Focus and the Result: The Neighbor and Love

We know that the cross deals with our need in holy vocation to die to ourselves, but for what purpose? The answer is so that we live in love. At the same time, "our interest is not in our love, it is our neighbor and the vocation to which our interest is directed."[85] "Love discovers for itself what is the greatest benefit to a neighbor."[86] But again, the Christian is not preoccupied with the thought of loving but rather the needs of his neighbor in front of him.

In *The Bondage of the Will*, Luther wrote, "But the children of God do good with a will that is disinterested, not seeking any reward, but only the glory and will of God, and being ready to do good even if—an impossible supposition—there were neither a kingdom nor a hell."[87]

That is, the Christian is disinterested in the good that love produces but is rather enveloped in their neighbor. Christians *lose themselves* in their neighbor. What do we mean? The Christian loses what the sinful nature wants: self-aggrandizement, credit for doing good, and serving pride and egotism that wants others to see their great love. Such sinful preoccupation is crucified.

All that matters to the new man upon whom shines the light of Christ are the needs of the neighbor. St. Paul wrote to the Galatians, "Bear one another's burdens, and so fulfill the law of Christ" (Galatians 6:2). And which Law was that? Jesus said to His disciples, "A new

---

85   Wingren, *Luther on Vocation*, 44.

86   Wingren, *Luther on Vocation*, 49.

87   AE 33:153.

commandment I give to you, that you love one another: just as I have loved you, you also are to love one another" (John 13:34). Yet again, we do not love to get from the neighbor, but rather the Christian becomes so consumed in giving to the neighbor that without even thinking about it, love is born.

Thus, the order is important: neighbor first and then love, which is reminiscent of another order: Christ first and then faith. To see Christ is to be given faith, and to see the neighbor is to be given love. If anyone wants to find faith, he should not go looking for faith, but find Christ and He will create faith. If anyone wants to find love, she should not go looking for love, but find the neighbor and God will create love too. All of this comes from the light of Christ.

Luther emphasizes the focus of new lives in Christ:

> Man, however, needs none of these things for his righteousness and salvation. Therefore he should be guided in all his works by this thought and contemplate this one thing alone, that he may serve and benefit others in all that he does, considering nothing except the need and the advantage of his neighbor.[88]

Luther also described the results of such preoccupation with our neighbor: the Christian now "serves one's neighbor willingly and takes no account of gratitude or ingratitude, of praise or blame, of gain or loss."[89] What is really occurring is indeed the miracle we mentioned above: "Each [Christian] should become as it were a Christ to the other that we may be Christs to one another and Christ may be the same in all, that is, that we may be truly Christians."[90]

In this light of Christ, we discover the significance of our horizontal calls. And we discover a common horizontal call within all other horizontal calls: to live in Christian love. As Albrecht Peters puts forth: "[This] should be part and parcel of all personal relationships and

---

88   AE 31:365.
89   AE 31:367.
90   AE 31:367–68.

should energize them."[91] Peters describes the impetus. It is outward. No longer is sanctification about going inside. "Such giving of oneself with abandon seeks to be lived out in the common ordinary events of everyday life, through and in all the personal relationships that mark various stations in life and offices."[92]

Our Gifts and Abilities Are Now at God's Disposal

Luther describes the Christian as taking note of their God-given gifts. When we recognize our gift, then God's will is straightforward: "You [are] to take this gift and serve your neighbor with it."[93] The Lord permits this distribution of gifts among His people "in order that he may test us and see whether we fear him and are willing to serve him therein and thus humble ourselves."[94]

Badcock makes the consideration of gifts a very practical matter, and in this self-evaluation, which can also benefit from the insights of those who know us best, we are led by the question "How can I best serve my neighbor?" "What remains is to find [what] . . . corresponds best to what lives in the self, to one's special gifts and qualities, within the specific circumstances of one's life."[95] And Badcock balances his counsel of how the use of our gifts is "capable of being integrated into the overall mission of Christ."[96]

Gene Edward Veith Jr. agrees that finding our God-given talents is important for "finding" our vocations.[97] At the same time, we must be aware that even our choices are "the overarching design of God."[98] So, while our calls are a function of our particular gifts and abilities, "our

---

91   Albrecht Peters, *Commentary on Luther's Catechisms: Confession and Christian Life* (St. Louis: Concordia Publishing House, 2013), 137.

92   Peters, *Commentary on Luther's Catechisms*, 138.

93   AE 51:349.

94   AE 51:352.

95   Badcock, *The Way of Life*, 123.

96   Badcock, *The Way of Life*, 136.

97   Gene Edward Veith Jr., *God at Work: Your Christian Vocation in All of Life* (Wheaton, IL: Crossway Books, 2002), 52.

98   Veith, *God at Work*, 54.

calling is not a choice out of many options but rather an assignment."[99] God chooses our callings. He places us where He wants us to be, and this is always for our good and the good of those we are called to serve.

When our calls are found and fully functioning, then we come to know a freedom not previously known. The light of Christ shining through us puts us where God wants us to be while doing what God equips us to do. It is another instance of the Lord commanding, "Let there be light." His horizontal calls also create, and in this, we are free to serve our neighbor with the light of Christ.

Thus far we have been describing what our horizontal calls are:

- They are the masks of God.

- They are "needed" by God as He appoints us to them.

- In them, we bear a cross.

- Through them, we are blessed and made free.

- They lead us to focus on our neighbor and live in love.

- They invite us to lay our gifts and abilities at God's disposal.

But what might we experience when we find ourselves living in them? How might people treat us? What might this response from others feel like? How will we know and experience God's help and strength to be faithful in our calls? To these questions we now turn.

---

99   Veith, *God at Work*, 159.

CHAPTER 2 DISCUSSION GUIDE

Christ's Light *through* Us
(The Horizontal Calls Understood)

UNCOVER INFORMATION

1. When God works through people, we call those people the _____s of God.

2. What is *the* biblical text regarding horizontal calls?

3. What unpleasant thing comes with every horizontal call?

4. Why are horizontal calls also great blessings?

5. Our crosses make us _____ to ourselves.

DISCOVER MEANING

1. If God doesn't *need* to work through people, then why does He choose to do so anyway?

2. Why is it appropriate to understand Christian sanctification (living holy lives in Christ) in terms of living out horizontal calls?

3. Why is the answer to question 3 above referred to in the way it is referred to (why we do we call it that)?

4. What do we mean by horizontal calls making us "free"?

5. What does it mean that if you want to find love, don't look for love but look for your neighbor?

Explore Implications

1. If God doesn't need to work through people yet chooses to do so anyway, why is this a good thing for us?

2. Who is the one really working through our horizontal calls? What does this say about the importance of them?

3. If we willingly bear the answer to question 3 above, it must mean the Christian is living for someone else? Who?

4. If horizontal calls free us, then what should the Christian say to the sinful nature that doesn't want to live in these calls?

5. If our neighbor becomes our focus, how are we released from gratitude or ingratitude, praise or blame, gain or loss?

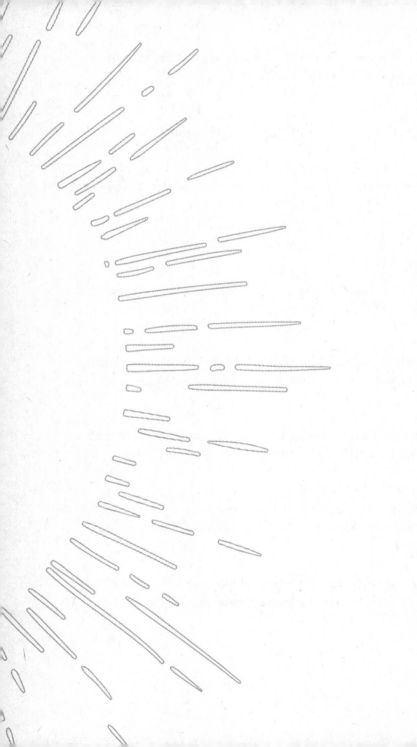

CHAPTER 3

CHRIST'S LIGHT *THROUGH* US (THE HORIZONTAL CALLS EXPERIENCED)

Treated as Christ Was

An inspirational highlight of camaraderie with the broader church is the March for Life in Washington DC, when Christians from throughout the nation, and representing many different traditions, gather to march through the National Mall. I've been blessed to attend a few of them with my brothers and sisters in The Lutheran Church—Missouri Synod while also preaching at the Life Conferences held in tandem with the march. When we march, we do not do so in protest of anything but in witness to the sanctity of life for the unborn and, indeed, for all people.

When Christians participate at such events, they are taking seriously the fact that their vertical call from God has indeed made them the light of the world. The shining of Christ's light speaks to the issue: the unborn, the newly born, people with special needs, the infirm, the elderly, and anyone who suffers are sacred in the eyes of God and are to be defended. Proverbs 31:8–9 says, "Open your mouth for the mute, for the rights of all who are destitute. Open your mouth, judge righteously, defend the rights of the poor and needy." The Church must shine this way to be the Church.

At one march, I had the privilege to march alongside a wonderful colleague and sister in the Lord. At the time, I was also her pastor before she later moved out of state. The day was gorgeous and the air crisp. Despite the cold, the sun felt pleasant on our faces as we were caught up in the exhilarating atmosphere. As we marched, we were singing hymns and spiritual songs. What a blessing to share this time with my sister in Christ and literally thousands of other Christians.

As we approached the Capitol Building, we were completely caught off guard by a violent attack. Someone from outside our column—perpendicular to us and running up to our blind sides—presented herself as a human missile into our ranks and then ran away screaming against us. This person made my Christian sister her target and hit her so hard that she went directly onto the pavement in pain and in shock. All of us were stunned. I came over to my sister to check her injuries and then helped her up. Her heart was pounding. We were there to shine for Christ but were accosted by darkness. We were there to do good, but then evil tried to stop us.

Our King of kings said, "Blessed are those who are persecuted for righteousness' sake, for theirs is the kingdom of heaven. Blessed are you when others revile you and persecute you and utter all kinds of evil against you falsely on my account. Rejoice and be glad, for your reward is great in heaven, for so they persecuted the prophets who were before you" (Matthew 5:10–12). And Christ taught His disciples, "'A servant is not greater than his master.' If they persecuted me, they will also persecute you" (John 15:20).

Jesus, the light of the world Himself, was not known by the world though the world was made through Him (John 1:10); the light of life was not received even by His own people (John 1:11); and many rejected Him and turned away from Him (John 6:66). Jesus knew what it felt like to be betrayed, spit upon, struck in the face, mocked, abandoned as He was denied (Matthew 26:48, 67, 68, 70, 72, 74), and all of these were but preambles to the false accusations, the flogging, the mocking, the nails, the cross, and the dying.

The apostles knew that it was not a matter of *if* they would be persecuted but *when*. And this explains why they assuredly did not pray that they *would not be* persecuted (since the Lord said they would) but rather that they would be steadfast and faithful *through it*. In Acts 5 we learn that the apostles were arrested. The ruling senate of the people of Israel wanted them to stop shining the light of Christ. They wanted the apostles to shut their mouths and stop proclaiming that Jesus was Savior and Lord. Peter said to them, "We must obey God rather than men" (Acts 5:29). And while those on the council wanted to kill them, they had them beaten and charged "not to speak in the name of Jesus" (Acts 5:40). How did the apostles respond? Acts 5:41 says: "Then they left the presence of the council, rejoicing that they were counted worthy to suffer dishonor for the name."

St. Paul wrote to St. Timothy: "Indeed, all who desire to live a godly life in Christ Jesus will be persecuted" (2 Timothy 3:12). For us in twenty-first-century America, perhaps we will never be put upon the pyre as some of the martyrs were, and let's be honest, we most likely will never know the persecution Jesus and the apostles knew, but there is nevertheless a tenor, a flavor, and a kind of partnership that all Christians have with their Savior in this world. Point blank: since Christians shine the light of Christ, they will experience darkness that tries to overcome it. Christians often feel like they are being rejected. In this way, they are just like their Savior, Jesus.

To be faithful to the Lord, who shines upon us through the vertical call to be baptized Christians and members of the Church, means we should never be surprised that what we get back in return are not smiles and pats on the back but just the opposite. I had a colleague in ministry who said more than once when sometimes good, practical gestures received administrative blowback, "No good deed goes unpunished." We must be prepared that the road upon which we shine Christ's light will be bumpy, swerving, and generally up and down. Where we belong in holy vocation is often not necessarily enjoyable and is most certainly not always a bed of roses. This comes as no surprise to us. We are treated as Jesus was.

Not Holding Our Breath for Recognition

St. Peter encourages us as we set out to reflect the light of Christ and when that light is not exactly welcomed by others. He wrote, "Finally, all of you, have unity of mind, sympathy, brotherly love, a tender heart, and a humble mind. Do not repay evil for evil or reviling for reviling, but on the contrary, bless, for to this you were called, that you may obtain a blessing" (1 Peter 3:8–9). Again, we reflect Jesus who "was oppressed . . . and . . . afflicted, yet He opened not His mouth" (Isaiah 53:7).

Christians must learn that they shine the light not for reward, not for recognition, and not even for reciprocation, but because that is who and what they are: the light of the world. With this view, it doesn't matter how people respond. With this realistic mentality, we know what to expect.

Wingren helps us to focus on the life we are called to and not the way people respond to it. "The human being also in his vocation serves his fellowmen, fulfills his task out of love for Christ and receives the same poor measure of gratitude as Christ did. This is the only way love of Christ can be real."[100] Along the way, Wingren reminds us that our vocation is "shockingly earthly" and "void of all divinity."[101] The divine light that shines upon us and through us must always be understood to be in the arena of the theology of the cross, where God hides Himself; it is not in the arena of the world's glamour.

Accordingly, the "Christian finds himself called to drab and lowly tasks" so that his sanctification in Christ "is hidden in offensively ordinary tasks with the result that it is hardly noticed at all that he is a Christian."[102] The lack of recognition and reward, in fact, can be so sharp that the Christian can easily be "tempted to do something other than his vocation, something that has more meaning and receives some measure of recognition from the world."[103] But the recognition of the world is here today and gone tomorrow. The recognition of Christ, however, is eternal. He knows when His people are living as He did. Of course, He does. He is living in them, making them beautiful even when the world sees nothing but what is ordinary.

Feeling Ordinary Is Extraordinary

I witnessed the results of a fascinating chain reaction growing up as a boy. My dad had become a mechanic par excellence. He received certifications

---

100 Wingren, *Luther on Vocation*, 31.
101 Wingren, *Luther on Vocation*, 57.
102 Wingren, *Luther on Vocation*, 73.
103 Wingren, *Luther on Vocation*, 171.

in Los Angeles and then Portland. By 1959, he was self-employed and in high demand in the great San Joaquin Valley of California. He was trained for the gamut: 18-wheelers, tractors, trucks, cars, you name it. He kept cotton-pickers running so that farmers could keep producing and maintained gigantic earth-moving Caterpillars for leveling the land that increased agriculture. In between, he kept big rigs hauling from field to storage to market. Talk about being a mask of God.

But the chain reaction I'm referring to was something only a very few people witnessed. Farm workers in the valley start working very early in the morning, but the equipment must be ready before they arrive. There was one person who would often arrive earlier than anyone: the mechanic. For us, that meant my dad was regularly getting up at obscene hours, but there was someone else quietly getting up with him: my mom.

My mom was there to help my dad prepare. Everything he needed: his clothing, coffee, and food, his lunch box prepared for later in the day; and whatever had to be talked about for the long day ahead was always covered between the two of them while it was still dark outside. Then my dad left, and my mom was left to run the household.

I've been around people who react to the hard work that goes into making homemade, fluffy flour tortillas, but because my dad loved them, there was my mom pounding away at the dough on the dough board with the rolling pin at 4:30 or 5:00 in the morning. That sound in my memory is a beautiful noise. It is the sound of one neighbor, my mom, loving and serving another, my dad. It was the sound of the Lord shining through my mom so that my dad would be enabled to keep doing what he was doing: providing for so many farmers (and as a result, the people they served) and providing for his family.

My mom was in the thick of it, but who knew? What recognition did she receive? She was never invited to the White House for a medal. She was not put in the newspapers for her extraordinary achievement in the home. Her service was quiet in this respect. It was hidden. She was like Christ. Her labor was hard. It had to be constant and predictable, it had to be consistent and reliable. She was always there to do it. Her service was extraordinary even while it could seem so ordinary.

In *The Great Divorce*, C. S. Lewis presents the writer in the book as having an incredible dream. He boards a bus and embarks on a journey through heaven and hell. In heaven, he observes an approaching procession with dancing light, the light streaming from persons in the glorious parade. In this amazing celebration was the "lady in whose honour [sic] all this was being done."[104]

The lady is shown in unbearable beauty, and Lewis's inference is that the writer in the story suspects that this lady was someone great on earth, but he is corrected by someone else in heaven who knows: "'Not at all,' said he. 'It's someone ye'll never have heard of. Her name of earth was Sarah Smith and she lived at Golders Green.' The writer then says, 'She seems to be . . . well, a person of particular importance?' To which the heavenly friend replies with, 'Aye. She is one of the great ones. Ye have heard that fame in this country [Heaven] and fame on Earth are two quite different things.'"[105]

We discover that this lady was "simply" someone who loved while she lived on earth. She had "sons and daughters" and even the beasts and birds would "come near her [and] had [their] place in her love."[106] She did not know the world's fame, but she was nevertheless "one of the great ones" and served those around her with the light of Christ.

It Doesn't Seem Fair

Luther presents the Christian way of life under two headings. The first heading presents the Christian as she is within herself, thoroughly hidden and often feeling "poor, troubled, miserable, needy, and hungry."[107] The second heading is the Christian toward others. In this outward direction, the Christian is "useful, kind, merciful, and peaceable . . . who does nothing but good works."[108]

---

104   C. S. Lewis, *The Great Divorce* (New York: MacMillan, 1946), 107.

105   Lewis, *The Great Divorce*, 107.

106   Lewis, *The Great Divorce*, 108.

107   AE 21:45.

108   AE 21:45.

This calculus doesn't work for the sinful nature. For the old man, we are not here for others but for ourselves. It seems unthinkable that we would give our best to others while we get the short end of the stick.

But this is where the new man reminds himself that he has already been through this equation before through something we call the joyful, the happy, the great, or the wonderful exchange. Jesus, who had all glory, gave it up and conducted a mind-blowing transaction: He gave us sinners His righteousness and holiness; His overflowing life and light *and then we gave to Him—while He lovingly accepted—our sin and guilt, our shame and misery, our curse and blame.* The Righteous One took our guilt; and the guilty ones (all of us) took His righteousness and innocence.

How *fair* was this for Christ? Fairness was eclipsed by the greatest love the universe has ever known. In this respect, fairness is beside the point. God's light overtakes the darkness of human reason and fairness. The Christian can keep giving, keep shining, because he will never lose what he has received from Jesus Christ.

For this reason, our heading of feeling troubled and miserable is covered by Christ's heading of the One who took our sin and curse; and our heading of useful and merciful servant is empowered by Christ's heading of the One who is always useful and merciful toward us. And what He gives us is inexhaustible. He doesn't stop serving us. This is the source of the Christian's strength and perseverance.

In all this, we are simply reflecting what we have received. And, in the meantime, we become like Him more and more in our lives sanctified in and through our vertical call, keeping us in our baptismal grace, and our horizontal calls, keeping us in imitation of Christ: living for others. From a worldly perspective, none of this is fair, but from God's perspective, it is the only life worth living.

Such a Christian living in this way "suffers in all sorts of ways on this account [as] he properly administers and carries out his office . . . to serve and help other people."[109] And it doesn't even matter which station among the myriad of horizontal calls we might consider. "No station

---

109   AE 21:53.

in life is free of suffering and pain, both from your own, like your wife or children . . . and from outside, from your neighbors and all sorts of accidental trouble."[110] In our holy callings, "it is inevitable that [we] should be offended, deeply and often."[111] As a result, "No one is satisfied with his position in life."[112] But we can't forget: more is going on that we do not see, so Luther wrote defiantly:

> So let us be shoveled under now and stay in hiding. The time will come when God will pull us out for our cause and our way of life to shine before the eyes of the whole world even in this life, but still more gloriously on that day.[113]

We Enter a Fight

To stay in hiding doesn't mean, however, the Christian is passive.[114] In Christ, he is also active. There is a good fight to be fought. St. Paul instructed St. Timothy as recorded at 1 Timothy 6:11–13:

> But as for you, O man of God, flee these things. Pursue righteousness, godliness, faith, love, steadfastness, gentleness. Fight the good fight of the faith. Take hold of the eternal life to which you were called and about which you made the good confession in the presence of many witnesses. I charge you in the presence of God, who gives life to all things, and of Christ Jesus, who in His testimony before Pontius Pilate made the good confession.

The Church Militant is in fight mode, but that doesn't mean Christians should be obnoxious, rude, or retaliatory. God reveals that our battle is not against people but stridently against demonic

---

110   AE 21:95.

111   AE 21:151.

112   AE 21:185.

113   AE 21:165.

114   We are to accept and understand our hiddenness, but this does not mean that we are hiding from shining the light of Christ against all darkness.

principalities and powers (Ephesians 6:12). We are to understand how spiritual forces working through people and the world will try to discourage us in carrying out our horizontal calls. Luther said that we have "good reason to become impatient, because the world is so infinitely evil and because [we are] . . . surrounded by snakes and all kinds of vermin."[115] But we mustn't permit our impatience to take us out of our God-appointed vocations.

Wingren is straightforward about these things: "[Man's] vocation is one of the situations in which he chooses sides in the combat between God and Satan."[116] When we are tempted to leave our posts given to us by God, "it is Satan who commands [us] to forsake men."[117]

Such forsaking leads to isolation, which pulls us back from serving the neighbor. As I wrote elsewhere, this malady leads to this kind of self-talk: "'It is just too much work to extend myself this way,' so the sinful flesh says, and in this way . . . individualism . . . join[s] the bandwagon of the end-times sign: 'the love of many will grow cold' (Matthew 24:12)."[118]

In holy vocation, Christians are fighting against the self-centered view that we are alive for ourselves. This urge to live for self is in the sinful nature of all people, including all Christians. We must begin by fighting the allurement within ourselves. "Temptation in vocation is the devil's attempt to get man out of his vocation."[119] He tempts constantly to make life all about *me, myself, and I.*

But the devil is a liar. What he puts before us isn't real. Veith is right here: "Whether we want to accept it or not, self-sufficiency is an illusion."[120] Our flesh, which wants the illusion, must be daily drowned in our once-for-all-time Holy Baptism and in this way be killed every day.

---

115   AE 21:223.

116   Wingren, *Luther on Vocation*, xi.

117   Wingren, *Luther on Vocation*, 54.

118   Espinosa, *Faith That Engages the Culture*, 237.

119   Wingren, *Luther on Vocation*, 121.

120   Veith, *God at Work*, 41.

Early on in my preparation for the pastoral ministry, I had the opportunity to serve dozens of congregations through a collegiate ministry team program over three years and then later through three different internships. In every case, when embarking in developing or fortifying youth ministries, we sought to identify congregational volunteers who would become the foundation of these programs. At the end of the day, while pastors assist parents in the training of their children, they never take the place of parents. To say the least, parental participation in youth ministry is invaluable.

I was always excited to meet young families who were eager to take the bull by the horns and jump into helping cover the nuts and bolts of programming. I met such a family that made me grateful for how the Lord provides for the practical needs of the ministry. They were a young couple, energetic and hands on, and had two adorable young children.

We worked together like a charm, and I was thankful for the team that we had formed. It was a lot of work but fun at the same time, and most importantly, it was paying off for the local congregation. We were reaching kids and families with the Gospel. Then, in the blink of an eye, everything changed.

From where I was sitting, someone had flipped a switch on the heart and mind of one of the spouses, and you could see it all over their face and hear it in their voice. They announced to me that they were fed up and done. They were sick and tired of putting everyone else ahead of themselves. Not only did they quit the youth ministry we had started, but they quit their spouse, their children, and their church. They left everyone and everything.

Unfortunately, this script has been played out much too frequently. It is a recurring nightmare that leads to children with broken hearts and the false expectation that the next person or lover will make everything in life better. It doesn't work.

It was a renunciation of God's holy horizontal calls. It was the turning away from the stations God had placed upon this one who had once professed Christ. It was a betrayal and a trading of Christ's light in vocation for the darkness and thirst of the world and the flesh. It was a shocking and sobering experience for me and taught me never to assume that those who are already in the church are safe and secure while still in this world. The fight must *always* be fought.

Wingren reminds us that for the person "who in truth loves only himself, vocation becomes rigid, unyielding, and coercive."[121] When faith and love leave, the neighbor—even if that neighbor is the closest family member—becomes repulsive and representative of a prison, shutting down our desire to be free to live for ourselves.

This is the view in the world and within us that we must resist and fight against. The fight is alarming to say the least, and it ushers us—by God's loving and merciful providence—to seek His help. This struggle is the fight we enter in our holy call and calls. "For a Christian desperation and inner freedom alternate, and between them stands prayer which changes everything, because in it, God is creatively present. Cross and despair come together in vocation, and drive man to prayer."[122]

Our horizontal calls bless us because they lay a cross on our sinful nature so that we would remember our need to cry out to God, to be incessant in prayer and constant in receiving God's means of grace. And our horizontal calls bless us because when we see how the Lord works through these portals of light, we learn to rejoice in His help that brings an order to know how to truly love. In the meantime, Christians welcome the fight; it means that we have a living faith that will not succumb to the temptation to run away.

Our Help and Strength

The great Helper and Comforter of the Church is the Holy Spirit.

Jesus said, "But the Helper, the Holy Spirit, whom the Father will send in My name, He will teach you all things and bring to your remembrance all that I have said to you" (John 14:26). To put it plainly, the Holy Spirit saves us in our fight against our sin, the world, and the devil, by keeping Jesus in front of our eyes of faith. And yet even the Holy Spirit Himself is part of the hiddenness of God in us. Luther says it this way:

---

121   Wingren, *Luther on Vocation*, 100.
122   Wingren, *Luther on Vocation*, 119.

> Externally there is not much difference between the Christian
> and another socially upright human being. The works of the
> Christian are cheap in appearance: He does his duty accord-
> ing to his calling; he rules the commonwealth, he runs the
> household; he tills the field; he helps, supports, and serves his
> neighbor. The unspiritual man does not praise these works
> but thinks of them as common and as nothing, as something
> that laymen and even heathen do. For the world does not per-
> ceive the things of the Spirit of God (1 Cor. 2:14). . . . Therefore
> there is nothing that the world believes less than that we have
> the Holy Spirit."[123]

But the world doesn't have to see the work of the Holy Spirit in us
through Christ's Word and Sacrament for His work to be effective and
powerful in us. The world cannot see our faith that sees Christ before us.
And this is just the way God wants it. Remember, the Lord is constantly
training us to walk by faith and not by sight (2 Corinthians 5:7). But
as for what happens within and hidden from the world is "Jesus, the
founder and perfecter of our faith" (Hebrews 12:2).

What follows is probably the best counsel any Christian could
receive. When you are in the midst of the fight and tempted to leave
your calling, what should you do? Pray to the Lord and then receive
the Word that puts Christ before you.

> If pain or sickness afflicts you, consider how paltry this is in
> comparison with the thorny crown and the nails of Christ. If
> you are obliged to do or to refrain from doing things against
> your wishes, ponder how Christ was bound and captured and
> led hither and yon. If you are beset by pride, see how your Lord
> was mocked and ridiculed along with criminals. If unchastity
> and lust assail you, remember how ruthlessly Christ's tender
> flesh was scourged, pierced, and beaten. If hatred, envy, and
> vindictiveness beset you, recall that Christ, who indeed had
> more reason to avenge himself, interceded with tears and cries

---

123   AE 26:376.

for you and for all his enemies. If sadness or any adversity, physical or spiritual, distresses you, strengthen your heart and say, "Well, why should I not be willing to bear a little grief, when agonies and fears caused my Lord to sweat blood in the Garden of Gethsemane?"[124]

In every instance, the strength to faithfully remain in our horizontal calls is the life of Christ. It is for us to keep fighting the good fight, turning from darkness and being conformed to light incarnate. To have the light of Christ shine through us means that we will be treated as He was, and this will demand patience; that our extraordinary status will feel patently ordinary, while every inkling of our old man will object "not fair!" These things are necessary since God uses them to teach us to rely upon His Spirit, who keeps Jesus before our eyes of faith.

The new question before us now is "Where?" *Where* has God ordained Christ's light to shine through us? It is time for us to consider the three estates.

---

124   AE 42:13–14.

CHAPTER 3 DISCUSSION GUIDE

Christ's Light *through* Us
(The Horizontal Calls Experienced)

UNCOVER INFORMATION

1. How was Christ received and treated by the world?

2. Why do Christians shine Christ's light in their horizontal calls?

3. How do Christians often feel within themselves?

4. In what way is the Christian very active in horizontal callings?

5. If a person only loves themselves, how will they view horizontal callings?

DISCOVER MEANING

1. The disciples left the presence of the council after being beaten rejoicing (Acts 5:41). Why?

2. How does the fact that God hides Himself help us to understand that even the Christian's sanctification is hidden?

3. What is the joyful, happy, great, and wonderful exchange?

4. Why are we constantly choosing sides between God and Satan?

5. Why is prayer so important in the middle of the fight to be faithful in horizontal callings?

EXPLORE IMPLICATIONS

1. How should the Christian serious about shining Christ's light expect to be treated at times?

2. If the Christian is not looking for recognition while they serve their neighbor, then what are they looking for while serving?

3. When we take the wonderful exchange into consideration, how does this help us with the concept of fairness?

4. Why are excessive individualism and self-sufficiency so dangerous to faithfulness in vocations?

5. Since the Christian has the help and strength of the Holy Spirit, what will always be kept in front of eyes of faith?

PART II

Christ's Light for the World:
The Three Estates

CHRIST'S LIGHT IN THREE ESTATES

Life Beautifully Arranged by God

Christian theologians refer to three categories in which Christians shine as the light of the world. These categories are typically referred to as "estates," or "realms," or "orders," or "hierarchies."[125] The tricky part is that the terms have been around for a long time and language develops and changes. What we *don't* mean by these terms are man-made institutions. They are rather God's way of making sense of life for us so that our lives are so arranged that they are beautiful, most certainly, at least, in the sight of God.

Indeed, for the sake of clarity it might be better to refer to these three as "mandates" or "ordinances" to convey what God has created and established for the sake of our well-being as His people.[126] In addition, these mandates of God's creation become *our* mandates from God on how to live. Since they are from God, all of them are good and holy. Furthermore, because the Christian takes his faith and love with him wherever he goes, there can be no shifting between the "secular" and "spiritual." While the Christian lives in the world, every estate is both secular *and* spiritual. Faith in Christ, active in love, makes all estates spiritual, regardless of how mundane or secular they might appear or feel.

---

125   Peters, *Commentary on Luther's Catechisms*, 119. Though Peters presents the order slightly differently, I start with "estates" to be consistent with subtitles in this book.

126   In his great work *Ethics* (New York: First Touchstone Edition, 1995), Dietrich Bonhoeffer argues that what we refer to as an estate is better described as a mandate. Either way, these are divinely established and real.

Where has God created and established these? This is a simple biblical summary that speaks the three estates into existence:

- **Family Estate:**
  "Therefore a man shall leave his father and his mother and hold fast to his wife, and they shall become one flesh." (Genesis 2:24)
  and
  "Male and female He created them. And God blessed them. And God said to them, 'Be fruitful and multiply and fill the earth.'" (Genesis 1:27–28)

- **Church Estate:**
  "And let us consider how to stir up one another to love and good works, not neglecting to meet together, as is the habit of some, but encouraging one another, and all the more as you see the Day drawing near." (Hebrews 10:24–25)
  and
  "Remember the Sabbath day, to keep it holy." (Exodus 20:8)

- **State Estate:**
  "Let every person be subject to the governing authorities. For there is no authority except from God, and those that exist have been instituted by God." (Romans 13:1)[127]
  and
  "Six days you shall labor and do all your work." (Exodus 20:9)

Not the Same as "Two Kingdoms"

If you've heard of the terminology "two kingdoms," then be aware that it is a different theological and biblical category that rightly points out that God leads through *power* on the one hand (think government) and *grace* on the other (think Church).[128] However, "Church" in the

---

127 Government is not synonymous with state. Government consists of authorities who serve the people, while the state consists of all people in a vast array of societal and cultural occupations, whether they are in positions of authority or not.

128 See chapter 9, "The Lutheran Lens—Where Are We," in my volume *Faith That Sees through the Culture* (St. Louis: Concordia Publishing House, 2018), 160–88.

kingdom of grace—in the "two kingdoms" model—is the Church in its narrow or most holy sense: the place where God gives the forgiveness of sins through the Word and Sacraments of Jesus Christ. In this strict sense, Jesus said, "My kingdom is not of this world" (John 18:36). In this kingdom, Christians are united to Christ in the *mystical union* and receive Christ through His *sacramental presence* in Holy Communion. These realities surpass societal constructs and functions.

On the other hand, and getting back to the subject of this chapter, when referring to the church under the heading of the three estates, *the church consists of the visible gatherings and local faith communities typically referred to as "congregations."* What makes the three estates unique in the discussion is that *all three* estates—family, church, and state—have *both* secular and spiritual aspects.

One of our interests in this volume is to understand how the estate of the church not only shines Christ's light upon the people within herself but also how congregations shine the light of Christ upon the other two estates. It is exciting also to consider reciprocation: how the estates of family and state also shine the light of Christ back upon the church estate. All three function with their unique purposes and contributions.

When it comes to the Church visible *and* invisible, is there any overlap between the two kingdoms and the three estates? There most certainly is, but it is beyond the purview of this volume to examine this, though a simple summary is in order.[129]

---

129   The overlap is real and in accord with the Word of God (e.g., the fellowship of Christians in Corinth was identified as "the Body of Christ," or the Church [1 Corinthians 12], which received the true body of Christ in the Holy Supper [1 Corinthians 11]). The Church invisible, one with Christ and the heavenly host, is also identified with and connected to the visible Church on earth, which is the assembly of God's people around the Word and Sacraments of Jesus Christ. Where true Christians gather to receive Christ on earth, there the true Church, which is also glorious, exists. We express as much in the Proper Preface of the sacred liturgy that leads up to the Sanctus in the Divine Service: "Therefore with angels and archangels and with all the company of heaven we laud and magnify Your glorious name, evermore praising You and saying: [then follows the Sanctus]."

Each Estate Needs the Other Two

All the estates are necessary. Each estate fulfills human needs that the others cannot. Furthermore, the three estates are designed by God to complete each other as they are intended to work in concert for maximal peace and order.

If the estate of family diminishes, not only are the estates of church and state harmed, but people who try to live in the other two (or only one) as if they comprised all of life will experience a hole in their lives whether they are aware of it or not. Something will always be missing, and things will never be right. This will be true not only for the individual but for the entire society, and would also be true if *any* of the three estates deteriorate or, worse, disappear. God has designed us to need what each estate is supposed to provide.

Christians Live in All Three Estates 24/7

Recall that we mentioned the challenge in terminology and the fact that we most definitely want to avoid treating "estate" as a man-made institution. What such thinking does is create the impression that we might walk from one estate into another depending on our activity at any given day or moment, as if walking out of our house meant we were temporarily signing off from the family estate.

Much to the contrary, what God has given us means, for example, that a Christian woman might *simultaneously* be a wife and mother 24/7, a psychologist 24/7, and an American citizen 24/7. Beyond extenuating circumstances, there is never a moment during the week that she is not all three at the same time.

Complementary, Not Contradictory

Luther recognized, however, that this requires the need for Christians to learn how to live almost as if they were different "persons that [they] must carry simultaneously on earth."[130] In many instances, Christians will not feel as though what they are doing is very *Christian*, but it *will be* just as much of God, good, holy, and necessary as anything else they

---

130   AE 21:110.

do. Luther wrote, "A Christian may carry on all sorts of secular business with impunity—not as a Christian but as a secular person—while his heart remains pure in his Christianity, as Christ demands."[131] The reformer offered an important elaboration:

> Thus when a Christian goes to war or when he sits on a judge's bench, punishing his neighbor, or when he registers an official complaint, he is not doing this as a Christian, but as a soldier or a judge or a lawyer. At the same time he keeps a Christian heart. He does not intend anyone any harm, and it grieves him that his neighbor must suffer grief. So he lives simultaneously as a Christian toward everyone, personally suffering all sorts of things in the world, and as a secular person, maintaining, using, and performing all the functions required by the law of his territory or city, by civil law, and by domestic law.[132]

The US military has had a robust chaplaincy since the eighteenth century. Chaplains, of course, are pastors who serve as officers in the military. Already in the simple definition just noted, we see the duality coming out: pastor + officer = chaplain (and one does not have to be in the military to know the duality). As I came upon the second half of seminary, Traci and I were open to the possibility of my becoming a chaplain in the US Army or Navy. In 1989, I took the oath in becoming an officer in the US Army, serving as a chaplain candidate.

At the time, US Army chaplain training school was in Fort Monmouth, New Jersey. I attended there the summer before starting my regular internship for the pastoral ministry. It was a fantastic experience, and I was proud to wear the uniform. But beyond the gas chamber, the early morning runs, the concentration course complete with .50-caliber bullets whirling overhead while we crawled in the dirt, learning about maps, backpacks, and MREs, the eye-opening classroom instruction, and the experience of making friends from all over the ecclesiastical map, there was one moment that made an indelible impression on me.

---

131   AE 21:113.
132   AE 21:113.

All the chaplain candidates had been gathered into an auditorium. We were going to be visited by the base commander. Of course, as he came down the aisle, we all stood at attention and saluted. He told us to sit and made it crystal clear that there was one thing all of us had to understand about being in the US Army. The general could not have been more blunt: "The army exists to *kill* people." He needed the chaplain candidates to understand *this one thing* so that if anyone had a crisis of conscience about this one thing, then they had better get out *immediately.*

I would eventually opt out of the army, receiving an honorable discharge, but my reason for leaving had nothing to do with what the general had said. I still hold a deep admiration for military chaplains who bring the saving and comforting Gospel of Jesus Christ to the men and women who serve our nation in the armed forces. I could have stayed, because if one understands the three estates, then one can be both a Christian and serve in the military at the same time.

Luther explained:

> A Christian should not resist any evil; but within the limits of his office, a secular person should oppose every evil. The head of a household should not put up with insubordination or bickering among his servants. A Christian should not sue anyone but should surrender both his coat and his cloak when they are taken away from him; but a secular person should go to court if he can to protect and defend himself against some violence or outrage. In short, the rule in the kingdom of Christ is the toleration of everything, forgiveness, and the recompense of evil with good. On the other hand, in the realm of the emperor, there should be no tolerance shown toward any injustice, but rather a defense against wrong and a punishment of it, and an effort to defend and maintain the right, according to what each one's office or station may require.[133]

---

133   AE 21:113.

The Lord said in no uncertain terms, "Love your enemies and pray for those who persecute you" (Matthew 5:44). He also commands husbands to provide for their families. John the Baptist did not insist that soldiers leave the military but rather that they not extort money and they be content with their wages (Luke 3:14). St. Paul gave St. Timothy direction: "But if anyone does not provide for his relatives, and especially for members of his household, he has denied the faith and is worse than an unbeliever" (1 Timothy 5:8). Often joined to provision is protection.

Early in our marriage, Traci and I had some vacation time and took a weekend trip to St. Louis with our infant son. We were excited about being able to spend a couple days in a hotel in the downtown area. In the middle of the night, I awoke to the sound of someone trying to get into our room.

I shot up and ran to the door. As I stood ready, sure enough, the door was opening from the outside! At this point, my adrenaline had me in fight mode. I slammed the partially opened door shut as hard as I could and then instantly opened the door wide having gained the element of surprise. The man standing there was holding his wrist with a grimace on his face in pain. There had been a mix-up, and he was thoroughly embarrassed and apologetic.

As a Christian, I felt for him and accepted his apology, and as a husband and a father, I knew I had done the right thing while protecting my family. Luther brings out the necessity of switching gears when it comes to living in our three estates 24/7: "Of course, a prince can be a Christian, but he must not rule as a Christian; and insofar as he does rule, his name is not 'Christian' but 'prince.' The person is indeed a Christian, but his office or his princedom does not involve his Christianity."[134]

Another Estate That Runs through the Other Three

Predictably, that last line above from Luther will challenge many Christians, especially in our cultural milieu that has willingly bred Christian nationalism or the idea that Christian faith must define the other estates. But it is also important not to take Luther out of context.

---

134   AE 21:170.

Recall that in outlining calls above, we made the important distinction between the singular vertical call, which makes us baptized children of God, and our many horizontal calls, which enable us to love and serve our neighbors in the culture. That is, there is ONE call that stands out from and permeates all the other calls. The call to be a Christian brings the love of Christ into all horizontal calls. The one call receives the light of Christ, and the others reflect the light of Christ.

Regarding the estates, there is something very similar going on. Albrecht Peters provides the clarification that there is another estate that is "admittedly not a fourth one, in addition to the other three; instead, it has pride of place as the central estate for a Christian person, to be lived out actively in all the other estates."[135]

Distinct from the ordinances or estates of the family, the church, and the state, is another: namely, the one *spiritual estate* or the *estate of love*. Peters says that this is analogous to the call of the Christian which "hovers" and is "saturating" the other calls.[136] So let's be clear: we do not list this other estate with the other three because it is above them, but at the same time, it is *lived out actively*, as Peters says, in the three estates.

In referring to the three estates, we note how Luther uses slightly different terminology and a different order, but it is clear that he keeps the three main estates together: "But the holy orders and true religious institutions established by God are these three: the office of priest, the estate of marriage, the civil government."[137] Luther explains why these are "religious" and holy: these "are found in God's Word and commandment."[138]

But Luther also recognized the highest estate, which has Christians *always* living in Christian love in all estates. Luther taught, "All Christians are truly of the spiritual estate, and there is no difference among them except that of office."[139] Through Holy Baptism, the Gospel, and faith,

---

135 Peters, *Commentary on Luther's Catechisms*, 112.

136 Peters, *Commentary on Luther's Catechisms*, 112.

137 AE 37:364.

138 AE 37:365.

139 AE 44:127.

all Christians are a "spiritual . . . people."[140] And here the reformer cites 1 Peter 2:9 and Revelation 5:9–10, which demonstrate that those in Christ are royal priests and kings.[141] The difference among them? Only that they have different responsibilities in different offices. What runs through them all, however, is Christian love. And this indeed is the one thing that involves all our estates with Christianity. Luther also knew this.

So why would Luther even use the terminology he did when he said of the Christian prince, "His office or his princedom does not involve his Christianity"? It is simply because sometimes the most loving thing to do while we serve in certain estates does not look like love nor, for that matter, even feel like love.

A Loving Father

Once upon a time, I was blinded by love and my brain went on vacation. My parents had seen me off to university (a very prestigious one at that), but just weeks after, I dropped out of school and arrived back home just in time to make my parents' jaws drop. I was greeted with, "What are you doing here?"

I boldly announced my plans to them. "Mom and Dad, I love [my then girlfriend] and we are going to get married." I will never forget that momentous reply and the sound of my dad's voice: "Not in this house." He didn't skip a beat. His response was immediate, stern, and sounded as if he were back in the marine corps. His position was in my face, defiant, and, if anything, sounded *mean*. He was my dad, but he was not going to help me with this one.

I was mad. He knew how capable I was. I had graduated top ten in my class in terms of GPA from high school and had proven myself able to hold down part-time jobs while demonstrating leadership and maturity in many venues. Of course, in my dad's mind, he probably would have said, "Exactly! Which is why I'm not supporting you on

---

140   AE 44:127.

141   AE 44:127.

this." At the time, however, I felt as if I was being betrayed. Family is supposed to back you up.

When I was in the middle of this life lesson so long ago, the last thing I would have told anyone was that my father was being loving, and yet as I look back, *it was one of the most loving things my dad had ever done for me.* I needed his strength and his position to shake me enough to realize I had made a mistake in dropping out of school and that it was not my time to get married.

My dad was being faithful to his call to be my father, not my buddy nor my cheerleader. He was, in fact, loving me in the exact way I needed to be loved at the time. Some call it tough love. So be it. It was a love that God worked through, and how I thank God that my dad didn't confuse his estates or calls. I needed my dad to be my dad. He was, and God blessed me tremendously as a result.

The point here is that all the estates are avenues for the estate of love, or the spiritual estate, but depending on which estate we are talking about, God's love and light *will be translated and manifest in different ways.* It's time for us to zero-in on how God's love is presented differently in the estate of the family, the church, and the state.

CHAPTER 4 DISCUSSION GUIDE

Christ's Light in Three Estates

UNCOVER INFORMATION

1. What are different ways of describing the realms in which we live?

2. What do we mean by the narrow or most holy sense of "Church"?

3. What happens to the other estates if one or more of them diminish?

4. Luther said the Christian needs to learn to live almost as if they were different _____s.

5. What is the other estate that runs through the three estates?

DISCOVER MEANING

1. Who established these? And why is this important to know?

2. How is "Church" in the two kingdoms the same *and* different as "church" in the three estates?

CHAPTER 4 : CHRIST'S LIGHT IN THREE ESTATES

3. If a Christian is a wife and mother, when is she *not* a wife and mother even as she lives in all three estates?

4. What does it mean that a Christian can conduct all sorts of secular business with impunity?

5. Why is this other estate that runs through the three called the "estate of love"?

EXPLORE IMPLICATIONS

1. What are the three estates God has established? Why are all three necessary for our lives?

2. The church as one of three estates is *both* secular *and* spiritual. Why is this significant for the other two estates?

3. Since all three estates are necessary, should Christians protect and defend all three? Why or why not?

4. Why may a Christian also be a soldier, judge, or peace officer and still honor God and serve the neighbor?

5. Why should we consider the three main estates as religious and holy estates?

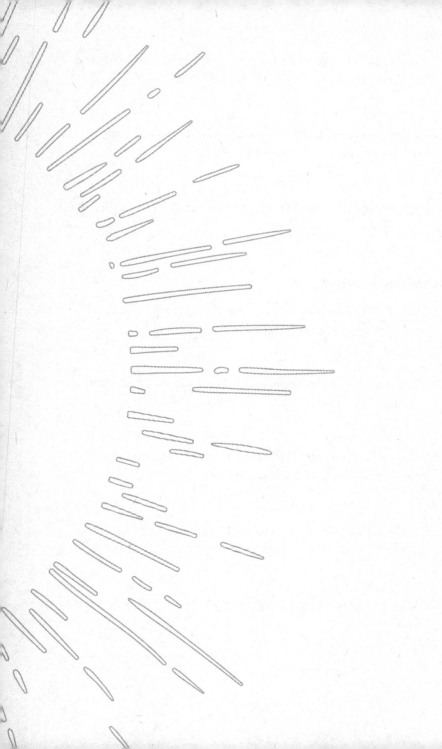

CHAPTER 5

CHRIST'S LIGHT UPON FAMILY, CHURCH, AND STATE

Estates of Love

To put it mildly, it is important to see *what* is conveyed by the light of Christ. To receive His light is to know *the love of God*. To reflect His light is to *love your neighbor*. Love envelopes any biblical consideration of vocations and estates. It is no accident that the spiritual estate is also referred to as the *estate of love,* as mentioned in the previous chapter.

This love, however, is also in the context of the difficulties Christians experience in their horizontal calls, which we discussed in chapter 3. This kind of love serves the neighbor despite the challenges that may dissuade service and turn us away.

There is a particular love that such descriptions refer to: we know it as *agape* love. It is the love of sacrificial service. It was the specific love that God had for us when He sacrificed His Son for us (John 3:16), and it is the love we reflect: "We love because He first loved us" (1 John 4:19). To be clear, the love in 1 John 4:19 is the same kind of love mentioned in John 3:16.

Point blank: this highest and greatest love serves the other *even when we don't want to.* For the Christian, it is sacrificial in the sense that we put our sinful flesh up on the cross again and kill all its temptations to turn away from the neighbor. Our sinful nature tells us, "They don't deserve it. Don't forget what they did to you!" Christ and our new conscience say, "I didn't deserve it either, but God didn't hold back His love for me, and my cumulative offenses against God are much worse than what anyone has done to me. Get thee behind me, Satan. I will crucify my flesh and love my neighbor anyway."

Agape and the Greatest Commandment

But before *agape* love is afforded to the neighbor, it is to be given back to God. The Lord Jesus Christ said, "You shall love the Lord your God with all your heart and with all your soul and with all your mind" (Matthew 22:37). God's Word says this is *the first and great commandment* (Matthew 22:38). Once again, the word used for *love* here is *not* the word for affection or friendship, nor is it desire, but is also like John 3:16 and 1 John 4:19, a form of *agape*.

This response toward God is not possible for sinful people. We are rebels against loving God this way, but by God's grace and with the help of the Holy Spirit, Christ loves in and through those joined to Him by Holy Baptism. Thus, while this love is impossible for the old self, it is also—at the same time—experienced by the new self insofar as we are in Christ. In other words, according to the flesh, Christians can't love this way, but according to the Spirit, Christians can and do.

Recall that when the Lord calls, He is not merely speaking a name or summoning but is bringing into reality what He is calling. When Jesus commanded Lazarus to rise from the dead, Lazarus did (John 11:43–44). Rising from death was impossible for Lazarus. Christ, however, made it possible.

When Christ calls us sinners to love, love enters the life of Christians even while they daily battle flesh, which opposes *agape* love. The greatest commandment, however, teaches us that the love the Lord shines through His people *pervades every area of their being.*

How the Lord presents that love is not random, but as Lenski says, represents a "psychological necessity" in respect to the order of heart, soul, and mind.[142] In giving the greatest commandment, God is also teaching us about how we are created and how we function as people.

---

[142]   R. C. H. Lenski, *The Interpretation of St. Matthew's Gospel* (Minneapolis: Augsburg, 1943), 880.

To be clear, in all the Greek biblical references of the greatest commandment, while each is somewhat different, there is still a basic order: we are commanded (which convicts us toward repentance) and, by grace, enabled (only in Christ's righteousness) to love God through the

Mind, soul, and strength (Deuteronomy 6:5 as translated in the Septuagint).[143] However, here the Hebrew for "mind" means "inner man" and "comprehending . . . will,"[144] so that the connection to the heart is clear.

Heart, soul, and mind (Matthew 22:37)

Heart, soul, mind, and strength (Mark 12:30)

Heart, soul, strength, and mind (Luke 10:27)

The heart is the center or the seat of our personality.[145] It is, as Gerhard Kittel analyzed, "the one centre [sic] of man to which God turns, in which the religious life is rooted, which determines moral conduct."[146] In the Old Testament anthropology, "it can represent life in its totality."[147]

In other words, the heart is indeed first in order. In fact, it houses the soul.[148] But the soul not only dwells in the heart but "is the consciousness of the heart."[149] And in the greatest commandment as recorded by St. Mark, "the soul here is close to strength of will."[150]

---

143   The authoritative Greek translation of the Old Testament.

144   Francis Brown, *The New Brown-Driver-Briggs-Gesenius Hebrew and English Lexicon: With an Appendix Containing the Biblical Aramaic* (Peabody, MA: Hendrickson, 1979), 523.

145   Lenski, *St. Matthew's Gospel*, 880.

146   Gerhard Kittel and Geoffrey W. Bromiley, eds., *Theological Dictionary of the New Testament*, trans. Geoffrey W. Bromiley, vol. 3 (Grand Rapids, MI: William B. Eerdmans, 1965), 612.

147   Gerhard Friedrich, Gerhard Kittel, and Geoffrey W. Bromiley, eds., *Theological Dictionary of the New Testament*, trans. Geoffrey W. Bromiley, vol. 9 (Grand Rapids, MI: William B. Eerdmans, 1974), 626.

148   Lenski, *St. Matthew's Gospel*, 880.

149   Lenski, *St. Matthew's Gospel*, 880.

150   Kittel, *Theological Dictionary of the New Testament*, 9:641.

C. F. Keil and F. Delitzsch comment on Deuteronomy 6:5, where the greatest commandment is first recorded in Scripture, and describe the soul for showing "love as pervading the entire self-consciousness."[151] That is, the soul bears great influence upon the heart. When the heart determines moral conduct, it will listen to the consciousness of the soul, and this will determine what is finally done.

The last of the three (or four in some cases) are "mind" and "strength." They belong side by side as resultant thought and action streaming from the heart and soul. The mind is the power to think and reason.[152] It is the last step leading to the activity of people. By the time we arrive to the mind, all has been decided by the heart and soul. People will think and act (while exerting their strength) according to what is in their core being.

Estates as Analogous to Persons

I've taken time to explain heart, soul, and mind because I'm suggesting that heart, soul, and mind provide a helpful analogy for understanding the three estates. How God has placed us and how God has commanded us to live in the three estates is complementary to and parallel with the way we are created. There is no complete person without a heart, soul, and mind, and there is no complete way of life without the family, church, and state.

What is more, both tri-sets are connected to God's love in Christ. God desires that Christians love Him with all their hearts, souls, and minds; and God desires that Christians love their neighbors in the family, church, and state. In this framework, *agape love* is the common thread. Luther says above that the three estates are the spiritual estate, which is "the common order of Christian love, in which one serves not only the three [estates], but also serves every needy person in general with all kinds of benevolent deeds. . . . Behold, all these things are called good and holy works."[153]

---

151 C. F. Keil and F. Delitzsch, *The Pentateuch*, vol. 3, Biblical Commentary on the Old Testament, trans. James Martin (Grand Rapids, MI: William B. Eerdmans Publishing Company, n.d.), 323.

152 Lenski, *St. Matthew's Gospel*, 880.

153 AE 37:365.

In respect to the three estates, however, order is crucial. I mentioned above that when the three estates are discussed in the literature, the order is often varied, but I have been deliberate and intentional about the order in this volume: family, church, and state.

How do we understand each estate in particular? As mentioned above, they all need the others and are complementary to the others, but what makes them different? By answering this question, we will have a better idea as to how the light and love of Christ are to be expressed. The analogy of heart, soul, and mind is offered to help us see the distinctions between the estates:

Family is the heart of the culture, showing its *character*.

Church is the soul of the culture, serving as a *conscience* and guide for knowing what is consistent with its Creator and what is not.

State is the evidence of the condition of the heart and soul of the culture, *protecting* and practicing what is at the culture's core.

There is no arguing that the heart is first; it is the center of our being, and it is wise to argue that the family is first among the estates as well. It is where everything begins biologically and formatively in every other way. "Train up a child in the way he should go; even when he is old he will not depart from it" (Proverbs 22:6). Any good psychologist will remind us about the crucial formative years of a person's life. What occurs and how a child is raised between birth and four years old will significantly impact how that person lives for the rest of their lives.

Keil and Delitzsch describe the love for God's commandments as first expressed in the home in the context of Deuteronomy 6:

But for the love of God to be of the right kind, the command-ments of God must be laid to heart, and be the constant subject of thought and conversation. . . . They were to be enforced upon the children, talked of at home and by the way, in the evening

> on lying down and in the morning on rising up . . . everywhere
> and at all times . . . [and] upon the door-posts of the house.[154]

But for this upbringing in the family to be good, then it must receive the conscience of the church. Recall that the Church in its strict sense is where people receive the forgiveness of sins, life, and salvation, no matter what is happening in the world. In this sense, the whole world can run amok, but not even the gates of hell will prevail against the Church (Matthew 16:18). In regard, however, to the three estates, the church is also secular just as the other two estates are also spiritual, so that the church brings a good conscience marked by godly virtues such as mercy, justice, and humility (Micah 6:8) to the other two estates. The church should unabashedly assert to the family and state realms what is good and what is evil and, therefore, what is to be embraced and what is to be shunned.

It is crucial that we are not, however, implying a merger of church and state. Not at all, but we are speaking of a balance. This was something I offered in a prior volume:

> There are reasons for maintaining the distinction [between church and state], and one of the most important ones is that the Church serves the state as a salve and conscience. Once the Church tries to marry the state, however, the Church will begin to lose her identity and in time will become a subcategory of the state.[155]

Indeed, each estate maintains its independence without merging with the others. Nevertheless, this does not cancel the inherent responsibility each estate has to avoid isolation and to actively extend itself to help and serve the other estates. Without this insight, an estate will suffer apart from serving the others. If, for example, the church estate is neglected, the other estates will inevitably hurt

---

154   Keil and Delitzsch, *The Pentateuch*, 3:324.

155   Alfonso Espinosa, *Faith That Sees through the Culture* (St. Louis: Concordia Publishing House, 2018), 169.

themselves and lose their consciences and drivers for good. When the estates are running as they ought to, they form a kind of ecosystem while maintaining their distinctive and unique purposes. For example, the state needs to realize it cannot create its own morality but must protect and preserve the other estates to avoid being swallowed up by its own power. The Lutheran Confessions take for granted this is true:

> Most excellent Emperor Charles . . . you owe the duty to preserve sound teaching and hand it down to future generations, to defend those who teach what is right. For God demands this when He honors kings with His own name, calling them gods, saying, "I said, 'You are gods'" (Psalm 82:6). They should work toward the preservation and growth of divine things, that is, the Gospel of Christ on the earth [Acts 12:24]. As God's representatives, they should defend the life and safety of the innocent.[156]

The estates maintain their distinctiveness in their entirety. At the same time, they enjoy a symbiotic coexistence. The church, therefore, will never try to make the government pursue Christian policy or Christian laws; it will, however, expect the government to maintain peace in the land so that the church may be the church.

In summary, to live in love in the family estate is to nurture and strengthen character that is trained in commitment and sacrificial service; in the church estate, it is to boldly supply the other estates with counsel and godly influence for holding to the good and rejecting the evil; and in the state estate, it is to responsibly care for, protect, and supply the other estates so that what is done in the state does not harm the family and church but continues to provide an arena that permits them to prosper.

---

156   Apology of the Augsburg Confession XXI 44.

The Estates Contextualize Our Calls

We now have a format for discussing the most important horizontal calls that reflect the light of Christ to our neighbors. Whatever is done in the family must show Christ as Father (think Isaiah 9:6), Husband, and Brother, who never leaves us and always serves us; whatever is done in the church must show Christ as Good Shepherd, who leads toward the good and away from the evil; and whatever is done in the state must show Christ as Almighty God, King, and Warrior, who preserves, protects, and provides for us.

Our *agape* love in the three estates will be marked by our lives in Christ in the ways that Christ serves uniquely in each estate. Again, we are reflecting what we have received. So, as Christ demonstrates His commitment to having adopted us and made us His heirs, we show His loving commitment to our spouses, children, and other members of the family. As Christ has showered us with grace in the Church, sharing His body and blood with us and imparting the wisdom of His Word to us, we share that wisdom with the world so that it would have light in the darkness. And as Christ rules the societal realm according to what is good and right, we love within the state as responsible citizens who help instead of harming others.

The Table of Duties Directs Our Calls

In Luther's Small Catechism, that section which is directly connected to our callings within all three estates is entitled "Table of Duties." It may be said that the Scriptures here presented not only command and instruct but also describe both the estate of love and the call to be baptized children of God. These duties are a picture of the Christian life and what love does.

Albrecht Peters informs that these "Lists of Household Responsibilities" were provided "so that everyone knows how he is to live and how he is to serve God in his station."[157] The table, however, goes beyond what occurs

---

157   Peters, *Commentary on Luther's Catechisms*, 109–10.

in the family estate and includes aspects touching on both the political and church estates.[158] Peters elaborates on their biblical foundations:

> The List of Household Responsibilities . . . reaches back to a point even before the Creed and the Lord's Prayer, to the [Ten Commandments], thus effecting a united presentation in the catechism; it characterizes the kind of love that flows out from the Christian faith and provides a setting for creative life within community, the . . . [practical application of the Gospel].[159]

Furthermore, the order of family, church, and state is also consistent. It starts "out in the house itself and projects from there out into public life."[160] The "household," therefore, is "a community for living and carrying on business, progressing outward, discussing the various stations in life within the framework of the three [estates] . . . [for] the all-encompassing Christian responsibility that one was to love the neighbor and offer petitions for the whole world."[161]

A Blessed Intersection of Family, Church, and State

Traci and I were inspired by one of my parishioners back at my first call in Covina, California. She was a foster mom and took care of many children, regularly and frequently bringing them to church. After we had our three children from natural birth, we prayerfully decided to follow her example and became certified foster parents.

This was first an experience with the state, and it was a good one. Through the state laws and procedures, we were properly prepared. In this case, the state helped us to make our home extra safe, complete with emergency evacuation plans and the locking away of medicines or anything else that could possibly harm a child. We were thoroughly trained for working constructively with birth parents or prospective adoptive parents and given an understanding about special needs of

---

158   Peters, *Commentary on Luther's Catechisms*, 111.

159   Peters, *Commentary on Luther's Catechisms*, 113. Second set of brackets in original.

160   Peters, *Commentary on Luther's Catechisms*, 114.

161   Peters, *Commentary on Luther's Catechisms*, 121.

foster children and potential treatments that might have to be maintained. We were also certified in first aid and CPR. No question, this experience demonstrated God's hand in and through the state for good. And this was a great blessing.

It was also hard work but extremely rewarding. We had several foster children, and, in every case, we had a "happy ending" in either being a part of the process toward reunification with the birth family or fulfilling the dream of adoptive parents to receive a child of their own. Once in the flow of the service to the foster children, I was also being called by God to be a father, specifically a foster dad. I now had the opportunity to serve the children as the head of my family. I was providing for them and teaching them. And this too was a great blessing.

Lastly, they came to church with us, and while they were part of our family, I was also their pastor. In God's house, they received His Word and prayer, and though we could not legally baptize them, we blessed them every chance we could get. This too was a great blessing.

The experience, however, was magnified when we could not find a home for our last foster child. After several months, Traci and I knew what the Lord was telling us, especially after having received the blessing of our daughter's birth mother: it was time for us to adopt our baby girl. This phenomenal blessing was facilitated by a new chapter in our relationship with the three estates. For example, we stood before a judge to make it all legal and official, and then nested into a permanent home, and finally, could now pour out—literally—additional gifts upon my daughter: as her pastor, I baptized her and later confirmed her.

All of this would repeat when we were inspired by God to adopt a sibling set of four. Four gifts from heaven, chosen by God and Traci and me. They became our children, and we became their parents. It would be a mistake, however, to even hint that we were the only ones giving and serving.

Our five adoptive children have probably taught me more about life than any experience I've ever had. And just when I thought I had parenting all figured out with our first three, the Lord humbled me, taught me to pray more earnestly, and made me stronger as a husband and father.

Through it all, Traci and I got to love our children in the three estates—complementary estates, yes, but all of them different. Through the state, we were qualified; through the family, we were refined; and through the church, we were covered by God's love and mercy. It all makes sense as I look back: God's Word guides our callings, and the estates teach us where the Christian life is supposed to take place 24/7.

A Framework for Shining Christ's Light in Our Horizontal Calls in the Three Estates:

From the Introduction: We receive Christ's love upon us (the vertical call), and now we are called to reflect the love of Christ to our neighbor (the horizontal calls).

Summary: *We reflect the light received from Christ.*

From Chapter 1: Our vertical call changes our lives (we are now in Christ and in His light), though it will not be as evident to us as we might like. Nevertheless, we can be confident that God will shine through us as He has promised to work good through all things.

Summary: *Christ's light is now ours, not obvious, but good.*

From Chapter 2: In our horizontal calls, as God shines through us to love and serve our neighbors, we bear a cross when faithful, but we are freed from living for ourselves and we now offer our gifts to God to be used for our neighbor.

Summary: *We bear a cross, but we are freed from self.*

From Chapter 3: While shining Christ's light in our horizontal calls, we will be treated harshly as Christ was, we will often not receive the recognition God's work in us deserves, our service will often seem ordinary and not exciting, and we will often feel our circumstances unfair. So, we enter a fight against our own flesh, and Christ keeps us in Himself so that the Holy Spirit is our help and comfort.

Summary: *We are tempted to leave, so we enter a fight.*

From Chapter 4: God beautifully arranges our lives and calls us to live in three estates: family, church, and state. We need all three for our lives to be right. We live in all three 24/7 and learn that the estate of love shines through all three of them.

Summary: *We shine Christ's light in three distinct estates.*

From Chapter 5: When serving in the family estate, we are living out the core of who and what we are. It is the heart of life and shines commitment and character to my most important neighbors. When serving in the church estate, I reflect the light of God's Word for directing all of life with a conscience to pursue what is good and to turn from what is evil. When serving in the state estate, I am shining Christ's light so that the state does not exist for itself but defends and promotes its heart and soul.

Summary: *Light and love are unique qualities that Christians bring to their vocations in family, church, and state.*

CHAPTER 5 DISCUSSION GUIDE

Christ's Light upon Family, Church, and State

UNCOVER INFORMATION

1. What is the particular kind of love that runs through Christian callings in all three estates?

2. What can a Christian tell himself when his flesh says about the neighbor, "They don't deserve my service"?

3. What is the psychological order of how we love God? List three things in proper order from Christ's command.

4. How are the three estates analogous to persons?

5. How might *agape* love be expressed differently depending on the estate?

DISCOVER MEANING

1. How does this particular love guide us in our callings even when we don't want to serve the other person?

2. What does our vertical call from Christ have to do with our ability to love?

3. What does the heart represent? What does the soul represent?

4. In using the human analogy, what is the family to the church and state?

5. Why would we say that a Christian judge is loving her neighbor by carrying out the law with a just verdict?

Explore Implications

1. How does 1 John 4:19 motivate us to be faithful in our callings?

2. If we are to love our neighbor, who must we love first? Why is this necessary?

3. How will the mind (and what we do) be affected by the heart and soul?

4. If the church estates serve as the conscience for the family and state, what happens if the church is silenced?

5. How must we train ourselves to love in the three estates? What must always be considered to answer the question "How do we carry out love?"

PART III

Christ's Light through Family Callings

Family
Vocations

Husband
and Wife

Parents
and Children

CHRIST'S LIGHT THROUGH HUSBAND AND WIFE

Horizontal Call above All Others

The family estate is the heart of the three estates, but within it, one call stands above all others: holy marriage. The day came when shamefully I forgot that. My wife was my rock through seminary, and I learned during our first years of marriage how important it was to lean on each other to make it all come together. She was always there to do that which was indispensable, whether caring for our babies, running the household, taking me through Greek flashcards, supplementing our income, or pampering me with delicious meals. She was also there to pray with me and to encourage me in ways only she could.

But when I became a pastor well into our marriage, I began to treat the office of the holy ministry as my most important calling. After all, this call was about serving sinners with the life-giving Word and Sacraments of the Lord Jesus Christ. People were being saved from death to life by the work of the Holy Spirit through the means of grace I administered in this God-given office. And it became my rationale for becoming a workaholic. The office itself had become an idol for me.

I was blind to the fact that I was flying by my wife left and right, too busy to care for her the way God had called me to do so. She became a bystander and spectator to what I was called to do in the church. One night, after coming home from another long, arduous day, I was completely surprised to walk into my entryway and be greeted by several packed suitcases.

Still ignorant to what could possibly be going on, I found Traci in our master bedroom. It was dark, but I could feel that something wasn't right. It was in the air. At a loss as to what could be happening, I asked her what was going on. She uttered five words: "You don't need me anymore." I felt as if I had been punched in the gut as I slid down the wall I was leaning on. It was her way of telling me I had lost sight of God's most important horizontal call in my life.

Our Horizontal Calls Are Prioritized

One of the reasons to see the organic order of family, church, and state is because this order also represents an order of priorities. But if the family is the most important estate in the culture, then marriage is the most important call in the family. This shouldn't be a surprise to us.

Timothy Keller reminds us just how important this estate is to God: "The Bible begins with a wedding (of Adam and Eve) and ends in the book of Revelation with a wedding (of Christ and the church)."[162] In between these bookends, marriage describes the relationship between God and His people (Song of Songs; Hosea 2:16, 19–20; Ephesians 6:22–33). Interestingly, the Lord's first miracle was performed at a wedding feast (John 2:1–12), while the kingdom of God itself is symbolized as a wedding feast (Matthew 22:1–14).

Marriage then is the perfect example of the fact that horizontal calls are prioritized. This is not for human pride for filling higher calls but precisely for the opposite. It is in God-given humility that we become cognizant of our weakness in the face of such holy calls. In this way, we become utterly dependent upon Christ so that we might live faithfully in the calls we are placed in.

If we are married, therefore, our spouse is our first call—recall we are discussing our *horizontal* calls, not our vertical call, which puts Christ above all things—and then after our spouse and if we have children, our children are next. For myself, my call as a pastor, as important as it is, will never supersede my calls as husband and father.

Luther provides a great description of the priority of holy marriage:

---

162   Timothy Keller and Kathy Keller, *The Meaning of Marriage: Facing the Complexities of Commitment with the Wisdom of God* (New York: Dutton, 2011), 13.

Therefore, [God] also wishes us to honor it [Hebrews 13:4] and to maintain and govern it as a divine and blessed estate because, in the first place, He has instituted it before all others. He created man and woman separately, as is clear [Genesis 1:27]. This was not for lewdness, but so that they might live together in marriage, be fruitful, bear children, and nourish and train them to honor God [Genesis 1:28; Psalm 128; Proverbs 22:6; Ephesians 6:4]. Therefore, God has also most richly blessed this estate above all others. . . . For marriage has the highest importance to God so that people are raised up who may serve the world and promote the knowledge of God, godly living, and all virtues, to fight against wickedness and the devil.[163]

After the Honeymoon

Gary Chapman is probably right in citing that *romantic obsession,* or what we might otherwise describe as "falling in love," has an average lifespan of about two years.[164] And we can hear all the people in the background saying, "Ah ha, and this is why it is a good idea to live together before marriage." That will seem true only if we go along with the cultural lie that marriage is all about personal happiness. Nothing could be further from the truth.

As Keller maintains, "The main enemy of marriage [is] sinful self-centeredness."[165] He elaborates, "Instead of finding meaning through self-denial, through giving up one's freedoms, and binding oneself to the duties of marriage and family, marriage was redefined as finding emotional and sexual fulfillment and self-actualization."[166] According to what God planned for us, "marriage used to be about *us,* but now it is about *me.*"[167]

---

163 Large Catechism I 207–8. Brackets in original.

164   Gary Chapman, *The Five Love Languages: The Secret to Love That Lasts* (Chicago: Northfield Publishing, 1992), 30.

165 Keller and Keller, *The Meaning of Marriage,* 15.

166 Keller and Keller, *The Meaning of Marriage,* 28.

167 Keller and Keller, *The Meaning of Marriage,* 29.

Recall that we enter a fight to be faithful in our horizontal calls because our culture is now characterized by what we refer to as excessive-, radical-, or hyper-individualism.[168] Our culture has tried to pull the wool over our eyes and whisper in our ears, "Life is all about living for yourself." This satanic deception is the worst enemy of marriage.

The Lord, however, knew what He was doing when He gave us the greatest family call of marriage. We may very well fall in love with the one we marry, but both husband and wife won't remain the same person. Both will change. Of course, here again is an occasion for devilish reason: "You now have an out-clause and a reason to get a divorce: *you've changed, they've changed, you both have changed.*" There you have it. End of story.

But this out-clause is for those who don't really know what marriage is. Before God ever instituted this holy estate, He knew what He would be teaching us through it. Keller explains, "Marriage changes us. Having children changes us. A career switch changes us. Age changes us. On top of everything else, marriage brings out and reveals traits in you that were there all along but were hidden from everyone including you, but now they are all seen by your spouse."[169] For this reason, when a person discovers the real love of marriage, they will experience a love that makes the wave of romance seem unworthy of comparison:

> When over the years someone has seen you at your worst, and knows you with all your strengths and flaws, yet commits him- or herself to you wholly, it is a consummate experience. To be loved but not known is comforting but superficial. To be known and not loved is our greatest fear. But to be fully known and truly loved is, well, a lot like being loved by God. It is what we need more than anything. It liberates us from pretense, humbles us out of our self-righteousness, and fortifies us for any difficulty life can throw at us.[170]

---

168 Chapter 3.
169 Keller and Keller, *The Meaning of Marriage*, 134.
170 Keller and Keller, *The Meaning of Marriage*, 95.

Therefore "wedding vows are not a declaration of present love but a mutually binding promise of future love."[171] In the present, however, we don't have to worry about the future, because of what God does when He brings a man and a woman together. Genesis 2:24 says, "Therefore a man shall leave his father and his mother and hold fast to his wife, and they shall become one flesh." God conducts something we never could. He makes the husband and wife one.

Speaking of Genesis 2:24, Keller refers to the "hold fast" in the ESV translation of the Bible as "cleaving," which is used in the older King James Version. What is being translated by these words is the Hebrew verb that means "to be glued to something."[172] This speaks to a commitment that is stronger than any emotion. Keller asks, "So what do you do?"

> You do the acts of love, despite your lack of feeling. You may not feel tender, sympathetic, and eager to please, but in your actions you must *be* tender, understanding, forgiving, and helpful. And, if you do that, as times goes on you will not only get through the dry spells, but they will become less frequent and deep, and you will become more constant in your feelings. This is what can happen if you decide to love.[173]

And this love, by the way, is the *agape* love considered above in chapter 5. The attitude of the Christian spouse becomes more and more like that of Christ. When the Lord Jesus was on the cross of Calvary, He didn't choose to love those who were mocking Him because they were so attractive while evoking warm fuzzies. Keller says: "No, He was in agony, and He looked down at us—denying Him, abandoning Him, and betraying Him—and in the greatest act of love in history, He *stayed.* . . . He loved us, not because we were lovely to Him, but to make us lovely. This is why I am going to love my spouse."[174]

---

171   Keller and Keller, *The Meaning of Marriage*, 87.

172   Keller and Keller, *The Meaning of Marriage*, 82.

173   Keller and Keller, *The Meaning of Marriage*, 104.

174   Keller and Keller, *The Meaning of Marriage*, 109.

Cross and Gift

We are reminded here as to one of the most important reasons why our horizontal calls are such a blessing to us: they pull us out of our sin-sick preoccupation with ourselves. They lead us to crucify our tendency to make it about *me*. Albrecht Peters would have us avoid underestimating marriage. It is true that "on the one hand, marriage is a 'secular estate.' . . . On the other hand, marriage is a spiritual, in fact a '*divine estate.*'" [175]

Luther teaches about marriage in his *Marriage Booklet*. In it, he guides how the couple should be prepared for marriage by the pastor. After teaching the couple that marriage is ordained by God, Luther emphasized three points:

1. The command of God concerning this estate (Ephesians 5:25–29, 22–24)

2. The cross that has been laid upon this estate by God (Genesis 3:16–19)

3. The comfort that comes forth from God's hold on this estate with grace and blessing (Genesis 1:27f, 31; Proverbs 18:22) [176]

Luther almost reads like a romantic when referring to his wife, Katie: "Though I may look over all the women in the World, I cannot find any about whom I can boast with a joyful conscience as I can about mine: 'This is the one whom God has granted to me and put into my arms.' I know that He and all the angels are heartily pleased if I cling to her lovingly and faithfully." [177]

Furthermore, in training his eyes to see his wife as a "divine gift and treasure," he learned how to put away the temptation to be unfaithful: "But see to it that you do not let such arrows (Eph. 6:16) stick there and take root, but tear them out and throw them away. Do what one of

---

175   Peters, *Commentary on Luther's Catechisms*, 144–45. Emphasis added.

176   Peters, *Commentary on Luther's Catechisms*, 177.

177   AE 21:87.

the ancient fathers counseled long ago: 'I cannot,' he said, 'keep a bird from flying over my head. But I can certainly keep it from nesting in my hair or from biting my nose off.'"[178] The command and comfort of marriage was to Luther all he needed to cast away the temptation to break the Sixth Commandment.

Still, Luther understood that a cross comes with the gift. Luther was able to elaborate on both realities. This was one way that Luther described the cross in marriage:

> If man and woman are truly joined in marriage, they do not have an easy time, for married life means labor and sorrow, or else it is not right before God. Wherefore, if in your married life you have to endure much sorrow and labor, be of good cheer and remember that it is so ordained that it is God's holy will that people should marry. Therefore in the name of God, I burden myself with trouble and give myself to marriage willingly and cheerfully. If you refuse to do this, and wish to do better, your soul will be lost, however well it may go with your body.[179]

But Luther also knew of the great blessing of holy marriage, so he also wrote:

> If we consider it in a godly and Christian way, the greatest thing is that on wife and on husband the Word of God is written. If you can look upon your wife as though she were the only woman in the world and there were none besides; if you can look upon your husband as though he were the only man in the world and there were none besides, then no king, and not even the sun, will shine brighter and clearer in your eyes than your wife and your husband. For here you have the Word of God that gives you your husband and your wife and

---

178   AE 21:88.

179   Marshall D. Johnson, ed., *Day by Day We Magnify You: Selected from the Writings of Martin Luther* (Minneapolis: Augsburg Books and Epworth Press, 2008), 297.

says, "The man shall be yours; the woman shall be yours. That pleases me well. All angels and creatures find pleasure and rejoice therein." For no adornment is above the Word of God, through which you look upon your wife as a gift from God.[180]

The Holy Family, an Example of Holy Marriage

The birth of Jesus happened in connection to holy marriage. We hear this gospel every year in the season of Christmas. Its details are important to say the least. Matthew 1:18–19 teaches that birth in the family is inextricably joined to marriage. This is the will of God.

In recording the birth of Jesus, the Savior of the world, Matthew immediately reports the fact that Mary and Joseph were betrothed. In the Jewish culture, this was tantamount to marriage. It was "stage one" of marriage, while the public celebration and private consummation represented "stage two." The betrothed among the Hebrews were already considered husband and wife.

We would be naïve to ignore the horrendous impact the deterioration of the family has had on our culture. God's Word shows us through the holy family what our culture needs more than ever before for healing and for hope to be restored. And healing and hope restored begins with the Christian family in the image of the holy family.

Joseph was the guardian and earthly father of the Lord Jesus Christ. He was truly a righteous man. Understand that Joseph had every reason to assume that Mary had been unfaithful. He was living in the betrothed state. He and Mary had not been intimate, and yet she was about four months pregnant when she returned to him after visiting her relative Elizabeth for three months (Luke 1:56). In God's Word, the sin of adultery for the Jews was punishable by death (Deuteronomy 22; Leviticus 20).

But note Joseph's reaction: not only did he have compassion on Mary to the extent that he would avoid her physical harm, but he went so far as to keep their divorce quiet so as even to preserve Mary's reputation

---

180   Johnson, *Day by Day We Magnify You*, 298.

and integrity. So what? Joseph epitomized what a Godly husband does. He is the guardian, protector, and supplier of his wife. The husband depicts true manhood by not allowing anything to hurt his wife. We hear St. Paul in the background in Ephesians 5:25: "Husbands, love your wives, as Christ loved the church and gave Himself up for her." We hear St. Paul again, this time in Colossians 3:19: "Husbands, love your wives, and do not be harsh with them." And then there is St. Peter's affirmation at 1 Peter 3:7: "Likewise, husbands, live with your wives in an understanding way, showing honor to the woman as the weaker vessel, since they are heirs with you of the grace of life, so that your prayers may not be hindered."

Strong and faithful husbands are just tuned in to doing what needs to be done for their family. When a wife knows that her husband is committed to caring for his family no matter what, she is blessed with immeasurable security and confidence.

This was Joseph. The Lord appeared to Joseph in a dream (Matthew 1:20) and commanded him to take Mary as his wife and informed him that Mary's conception was from the Holy Spirit. Joseph was instantly obedient. Later, the Lord instructed him to take Mary and the infant Christ to Egypt (Matthew 2:13). We read this as if it is nothing because we have cars and planes. Joseph instantly obeyed and did what was necessary for the 175-mile arduous journey to protect his family.

Joseph led his family out of the jurisdiction of the crazy king out for the blood of children because one might eventually threaten to take his throne. Later, Joseph would once again be faithful as he would move his family to Nazareth even while keeping up his radar for fear of what Herod's son Archelaus was capable of. This godly husband and father spared nothing to ensure the protection and provision of his family. This was Joseph, the guardian and protector of God in the flesh, and his holy wife, Mary, the mother of God.

What happens within a wife when she knows a husband like this? Such men do not need the limelight. They have nothing to prove. They just do what is necessary for their families. Joseph was such a husband to Mary. She must have seen God's light in her husband.

At the same time, Mary shone as a holy wife. It might seem obvious that there is no question that Mary instantly shines as the holy mother in receiving the annunciation from the angel Gabriel. Her living in the holy estate of family in the holy vocation as mother of the Christ was immediately embraced with remarkable faith. She replied to Gabriel's annunciation by saying, "Behold, I am the servant of the Lord; let it be to me according to your word" (Luke 1:38).

But what about shining as wife? Well, let's remember what we just covered about Joseph. Mary knew that he was also from God. Joseph would not have been able to faithfully lead if Mary had not faithfully followed. *Because she was the Lord's servant as she had told Gabriel, she would also be faithful in following her husband, Joseph.*

What did Mary think about her husband? She had a husband who avoided his legal right to have harmed her; who cared even for her reputation in a male-dominated culture; who was exemplary in his servant heart and obedience to God; and who sacrificed so much to do whatever was necessary to protect her and her Son, Jesus. Joseph anticipated what St. Paul would write sixty years later, "Husbands, love your wives, as Christ loved the church and gave Himself up for her" (Ephesians 5:25). Indeed, Mary must have held her husband close to her heart.

And this is how she innately teaches wives. Husbands do much to serve their families, but they need the respect, trust, and confidence of their wives. They are blessed when their wives affirm their servant leadership in the image of Christ. She understands the words given to St. Paul in Ephesians 5: "Wives, submit to your own husbands, as to the Lord" (Ephesians 5:22). This is not a begrudging thing but a free thing that is analogous to Christians submitting to God, or even better, Christ submitting to the Father.

Kathy Keller considers the words of Genesis 2:18, "a helper fit for him"—*ezer*—from the Hebrew. It is "almost always used in the Bible to describe God himself."[181] To "help" someone in this way is to make up for what is lacking in them with the strength the *ezer* provides.[182] In application to the wife specifically, it is like one who perfectly fits her

---

181   Keller and Keller, *The Meaning of Marriage*, 173.
182   Keller and Keller, *The Meaning of Marriage*, 174.

husband as in two half circles facing the other and then coming together to form a whole. Such an *ezer* completes the other as a counterpart or complementary opposite.

Kathy Keller recounts her own experience: "Let me emphasize that Jesus' willing acceptance of this role was wholly voluntary, a gift to His Father. I discovered here that my submission in marriage was a gift I offered, not a duty coerced from me."[183] The husband she says is like a servant leader who matches the wife who is a strong helper.[184] She's not wrong. The bottom line according to Holy Scripture is this: husbands sacrifice, wives submit, and both mirror the shining and glorious picture of Christ and His Bride, the Church. This is a marriage made in heaven.

The Greater Witness to the World

I was richly blessed to spend some time with Rev. Michael Salemink, executive director of Lutherans For Life.[185] I asked him about how faithful married Christians can shine forth the light of Christ in our world today, especially as we might try to build bridges to show the light of Christ. Michael was insightful about how the family estate, especially the holy call of husband or wife can shine in the culture:

> First, we as Christians celebrate the blessing of life and family that God gives us. We enjoy those so that instead of spending time running down our spouses or the burden of our children, we recognize that in a fallen world there are sufferings that come along with that, but the blessings that are mediated even in that suffering are so much greater, and we can confess those to people around us. You know when the fellas are out drinking and running down the old ball and chain that's an opportunity for us to say, yeah, marriage is a lot of sacrifice and difficult, but my wife has had to put up with as much if not more and I can't imagine life without her.

---

183 Keller and Keller, *The Meaning of Marriage*, 175.

184 Keller and Keller, *The Meaning of Marriage*, 185.

185 Michael Salemink, live interview by author, Zoom video call, July 25, 2022.

Secondly, there are common grounds, there are basic biological truths that still hold in our culture's warped understanding of relationships, of marriage and family, that God created us to be connected to other people, that we have a deep need to belong. I think that's still a common ground, even if it gets twisted. I think ultimately what drives cultural misunderstandings about sexuality, gender, relationships is that this deep need to belong to someone has been failed by selfishness in the world, but that doesn't eliminate the need; it just forces us to seek it in unhealthy ways, which leads me to a third way I see as a point of connection is that we as Christians continue to share life and life's blessings with the people around us. You know, Martin Luther was a genius for a lot of reasons, but one of the things that he saw was that the authentic Christian life is not one that is lived off in the monastery disconnected from people, but the proclamation of the Gospel is propagated as we intersect with people around us and as we share the blessings of life and family that God gives us. And I think that, as the world and the culture around us see the beauty of, sort of, Gospel-faceted life and family together, they will begin to see some of the bankruptcy of the substitutes for that. Because that deep-seated need to be connected to other people, not just to love but to be genuinely loved, is still there, and they are going to want what they see God giving to us.

The Rest of the Story

When Traci told me the truth I needed to hear, she did not yell and scream. She didn't attack. She went to great lengths, however, to get through to me while loving me. The way she handled herself led to my great benefit and help as her husband, and it is something I will never forget. But that's how Traci shows me Jesus.

Repentance is the way we get back to properly taking care of our calls. We believe, teach, and confess that it has two parts: contrition, as in "the terrors striking the conscience through the knowledge of sin.

The other part is faith, which is born of the Gospel [Romans 10:17] or the Absolution and believes that for Christ's sake, sins are forgiven."[186] We also acknowledge, "Then good works are bound to follow, which are the fruit of repentance [Galatians 5:22–23]."[187]

My wife's words cut to the heart, and I saw my sin. But she also forgave me and assured me that she still loved me, that is, she confirmed her ongoing commitment to our marriage even while it hadn't been great for her. And through this, I was moved by the Holy Spirit to respond with the fruit of repentance.

By the grace of God, we determined to make a major change that we have stuck to for decades now: my weekly day off would be a day for us. It was our date day. And, because my wife is not big on parties for herself, we are committed to doing something special for her birthday and then our wedding anniversary. Almost every time, we get out of dodge and spend quality time together on both occasions. This is much more than recreation and rest time for us. It is our commitment to each other to take care of our marriage.

This is what we do in marriage: we remain faithful through all the ups and downs of life. No pastor can preach a sermon about marriage better than a faithful couple celebrating many years of commitment in Christ. When this occurs, it often gives evidence that the soulish conscience of the church has influenced the heart of the family. God makes us one, and then we respond by living that out for the rest of our lives. Heart and soul are in concert.

This is also something the state estate desperately needs to see in our day. Life has become so transient, frenetic, changing faster than ever before, that the culture needs to see that stability and commitment still exist. There is no more powerful testimony than two who will stay together regardless of all the changes and chances of life. Indeed, this gift, this sacred call to be husband or to be wife, we must guard and protect.

---

186   Augsburg Confession XII 4–5.

187   Augsburg Confession XII 6.

CHAPTER 6 DISCUSSION GUIDE

Christ's Light through Husband and Wife

UNCOVER INFORMATION

1. What one horizontal call stands above all others in the family estate?

2. According to Chapman, "falling in love" has an average lifespan of about how long?

3. How does Keller say that marriage "liberates" us?

4. Marriage is both a secular estate and a _____ estate.

5. How did Joseph show his faithfulness as a husband?

DISCOVER MEANING

1. What are the practical implications of how horizontal calls are prioritized?

2. What does Keller mean that "marriage used to be about *us*, but now it is about *me*."

3. What does it say about the marriage vows that they are a mutually binding promise of future love?

4. How is the Christian to deal with the temptation to be unfaithful in marriage?

5. What do husbands need from their wives?

EXPLORE IMPLICATIONS

1. According to Luther, why is marriage so important?

2. In marriage, husband and wife change. Why is this a good thing for teaching us about the commitment of marriage?

3. What does "hold fast" say about the relationship between husband and wife? How does God view them?

4. Compare the two long quotes about marriage by Luther. What do these teach about marriage?

5. The wife is *ezer*. How does this help us to understand her calling? How should this impact the way her husband treats her?

CHRIST'S LIGHT THROUGH PARENTS AND CHILDREN

The Priority for Christian Parents

There was this one occasion I distinctly remember when my dad was getting after me, his rambunctious teenager, and he made one thing perfectly clear: he wasn't my friend or buddy, but my father. I might negotiate with a friend, but toward my father I owed obedience. That little moment in time paid off for me big time as Traci and I raised our eight children. And while I am playful at heart and understand the universality of friendship among the people of God (Christ, our Lord, calls us friends now, John 15:15), I was taught to be a father first for my children.

Interestingly, there is only one Scripture put under the rubric of "To Parents" in the Table of Duties. Ephesians 6:4 says: "Fathers, do not exasperate your children; instead, bring them up in the training and instruction of the Lord."[188]

Thomas M. Winger explicates the verse:

> As the husband was exhorted to exercise his headship with sacrificial love (Ephesians 5:25), so now the father is warned not to abuse his authority through excessively severe discipline, partiality, unreasonableness, or unjust condemnation; he is to exercise his fatherhood as God does (cf. 6:9). He is to

---

188 Small Catechism, Table of Duties, To Parents.

treat his children not as property but as fellow members of the body of Christ.[189]

St. Paul's instruction, though, continues in this single verse as fathers are also instructed "to act as blessings to their children in the way that God has given them to do. The verb [for 'bring them up' means] 'to nourish' [and] occurs in the NT only here and in 5:29, where it compared a man's care of his own body to Christ's care for his bride, the church."[190]

This loving nourishment providing discipline might "include painful correction and punishment . . . [but] is accompanied by . . . 'instruction' rooted in God's Word. . . . It is 'setting right the mind' through teaching, reproof, or warning."[191] And finally, because it is the discipline *of the Lord*, "the emphasis is more on the *teaching* duties of the father."[192] This kind of discipline makes a disciple, "that is, to put the Lord's *teachings* into the child. Paul's admonition is that the medium and the message ought to coincide, that the teaching be done with gentleness (2 Timothy 2:25) and love (Revelation 3:19), as God himself does."[193]

If anyone thinks this sounds easy, then they might want to wake up from dreaming. This is a startling call, and it should drive parents to pray. Luther offered one such prayer:

> Dear Lord, I have Thy Word, and I am in the station that pleases Thee. This much I know. Thou seest all my inadequacies, and I know no help except in Thee. Help Thou, therefore, because Thou hast commanded that we should ask, seek, and knock, and hast said that then we shall surely receive, find, and have what we want.[194]

189   Winger, *Ephesians*, 662.
190   Winger, *Ephesians*, 662.
191   Winger, *Ephesians*, 662–63.
192   Winger, *Ephesians*, 663.
193   Winger, *Ephesians*, 663.
194   AE 21:233.

I asked Michael Salemink about the importance of parents teaching their children the saving faith, and he said that the first thing that came to his mind was his responsibility as a father: "A father, a husband, has a responsibility as head of the household to model certain things to his family, to teach, especially his children."[195]

But while the responsibility is clear, it also runs against the grain of our culture. Michael pointed out that we must overcome the individualism of the day that can also spill over into our devotional life. We must ensure that it doesn't become "entirely private," so that "worship and devotion, becomes just between me and God. And that, of course, is not how the Lord intended it to be."[196]

Luther was lucid about these things in the Large Catechism: "Therefore, it is the duty of every father of a family to question and examine his children . . . at least once a week and see what they know or are learning from the catechism."[197] He also warned, "Let [every parent] know that it is his duty, on peril of losing the divine favor, to bring up his children in the fear and knowledge of God above all things [Proverbs 1:7]."[198]

We know the preamble to many of the parts in the Small Catechism: "As the head of the family should teach them in a simple way to his household."[199] How important did Luther think this was? He taught that if a child was unwilling to learn these things, that he or she should not be permitted to stay in the house.[200]

---

195   Salemink, interview.

196   Salemink, interview.

197   Large Catechism, Short Preface, 4.

198   Large Catechism I 174. Brackets in original. Proverbs 1:7 states, "The fear of the LORD is the beginning of knowledge; fools despise wisdom and instruction."

199   Small Catechism, The Ten Commandments. This is the preamble for the Ten Commandments; then the words are repeated for the Creed, the Lord's Prayer, the Sacrament of Holy Baptism, the Sacrament of the Altar, and the Prayers. The head of the household might be the mother of the children if the father is unable or unwilling to execute his call.

200   Large Catechism, Short Preface 17. Though this is severe, it is a far cry from the theocratic injunction to take the stubborn and rebellious son to the city gates for capital punishment (Deuteronomy 21:18–21).

The Cross of Parents

The cross in the call to be a parent might seem self-evident if for nothing else but the immensity of the responsibilities inherent in Ephesians 6:4. If marriage is hard work, then it is painfully obvious that parenting is as well. But the cross comes also because parents must bear the sin and suffering of their children.

The Christian father is to be as the Lord for his children. The father carries the children of his household. He is called to protect them and to provide for them. He fights for them. He is their first pastor. He disciplines them and showers them with love. Yes, this involves a cross, but it also means the father enters his children's lives. He shares their joys and victories, their fears and their pains. The struggles of the children become the struggles of the parents; and the pain of the children is felt in the hearts of loving parents.

Sometimes the pain we feel might just make us shake our heads, but other times it is visceral, and we can feel our hearts break in our chests. Sometimes what we feel makes us laugh, because if we didn't we would cry. Other times, we have no choice but to cry.

One of those five daughters I mentioned previously comes to mind when I think about sharing their lives and their precious—and unpredictable—ups and downs. She was only about three and loved to draw—especially with crayons. But one day, she was nowhere to be seen in the house. Traci and I started looking all over for her. When I found her, I almost passed out.

Traci and I had, for the first time in our marriage, financed a brand-new car, which—I believe—was the last time we did so. It was a current-year model, a dark metallic green minivan.[201] It sat, protected in the garage, sparkling new. It still *smelled* new. My little girl with gorgeous curlicue hair had found the perfect "board" for her creative—as well as indistinguishable—drawings. That "board" was the sparkly metallic sliding door of our van. But she wasn't using a crayon. She had found a pointed rock.

---

201   I still can't believe I once owned a green vehicle.

I didn't yell, but my gasp was so loud that she swung around. Her face at such a young age told the whole story: she was having a great time—truly—but she already looked guilty. The Holy Spirit had done His work. She was convicted.

I saw the look on her face. It was priceless. She was already sorry before I uttered a word. What would I impress on her even if she would never remember this escapade after growing up? I smiled at her, scooped her up, and consoled her. I poured grace over her while reminding her that we drew on paper and not on mommy and daddy's car.

Then came the time when she disobeyed and took the hamster out of its cage. The hamster bit her finger, and you know that fight or flight thing? Well, she decided to fight, and I had no idea how strong she was, because she flung the hamster across the room and the hamster was finished. She was upset now for many reasons. I taught. I consoled. Then I took all three of the little ones (we only had three at the time) and conducted a Christian burial for our dear hamster in the front yard.[202] When Traci pulled up to the house, she was wondering why the kids were staring at the ground bawling their eyes out.

In the blink of an eye, the same daughter was in high school, and I was her biggest fan. A father could not have been prouder, but she was neck and neck for being valedictorian of her senior class. When I learned that the other gal was going to get it because her extra music class nudged her .001 percent past my daughter, I almost lost it. I could feel my temperature rising in me for the injustice against my own flesh. She handled it much better than me, but I *had to* contain myself since I was teaching theology part-time at my daughter's Lutheran high school. This was one of those occasions for going to confession.

Then came moving her to university. As parents, we could not have been prouder, but as I walked away with Traci, I was crying. Not long after that, I was talking to my daughter on the phone. Something had happened that was so upsetting to her that her first instinct was

---

202   We thanked God for the hamster and withheld the full liturgy.

to come home. She insisted that she couldn't concentrate. I listened, I wept with her, I prayed with her, and I asked her for just one more day. That was the strategy: bear with her one day at a time, and the Lord gave her great friends to support her, and before I knew it, she was off and running again.

As I make the point about feeling what your children go through, bearing their burdens and in this way fulfilling the law of Christ (Galatians 6:2), I've used light examples, but what happens is not always so easy. I've been there not only for my own experiences as a parent but for the countless parents I've served as pastor.

When your child is being rushed in for emergency surgery, when he loses his way and falls into addiction, or even when she starts to see how cruel people can be, then we know the cross. We suffer under the cross with our most precious neighbors after our spouse and our dear children.

But recall that the cross also comes with a fight. The fight against sin: the sin within themselves, as well as the world, and the devil trying to destroy them left and right. Our children are also aliens and strangers passing through this world (1 Peter 2:11). Who will protect them, guard them, and fight for them? Welcome to your call if you are a parent.

Our Matthew 25 Children and the Blessing

In his 1520 *Sermon on Good Works*, Luther celebrates the blessedness of having children even while describing the parents' immense responsibility:

> Thus it is true that parents, even if they had nothing else to do, might attain eternal blessedness through their children. And if they bring them up in the true service of God, they will have both hands full of good works to do. What else are the hungry, thirsty, naked, the prisoners, the sick, and the strangers here but the souls of your own children (Matthew 25:35–36)? It is for their sake that God makes your house a hospital and appoints you the master of it, that you may tend them, feed them, and quench their thirst with good words

and works, so that they learn to trust in God, believe in him, fear him, and place their hope in him. This is in order that they will honor his name, neither swear nor curse, be diligent, worship God and hear his Word . . . bear misfortune meekly, not to fear death or to love this life! Oh, what a blessed home where such parents live. It is indeed like a true church, a select monastery, yes, like paradise.[203]

Leave it to Luther to round out things for us. Yes, parents have a great responsibility, and they will know a cross if they are faithful in raising their children, but the magnitude of the light of Christ in this vocation is staggering. Sometimes Christians consider passages such as Matthew 25:35–36 and wonder, "Am I really doing *that*?" Well, if you're a parent, the answer is, "Yes, because the Lord has made your home into a hospital, a church, and a paradise on earth." The Lord is causing you to conduct so many good works, you're not even aware of them. And that's a good thing.

Children Called to Honor Parents

Christian children also have a call not just to be served by their parents but to serve and honor their parents. Parents are the children's most important neighbors as they grow up.

Once again, this is a cross, since no horizontal call from God is without the holy cross. It is easily a cross, because to begin with, since we are sinful from birth and from the time of our conception, we rebel against the Fourth Commandment: "You shall honor your father and your mother that it may be well with you and you may live long upon the earth."

Luther asks in the Small Catechism, "What does this mean? We should fear and love God so that we do not despise or anger our parents and other authorities, but honor them, serve and obey them, love and cherish them."[204]

---

203   Johnson, *Day by Day We Magnify You*, 65.
204   Small Catechism, Fourth Commandment.

The Fourth Commandment "is the first and greatest" among the Fourth through Tenth Commandments.[205] Luther wrote, "To the position of fatherhood and motherhood God has given special distinction above all positions that are beneath it: He does not simply command us to love our parents, but to honor them."[206]

To honor and not merely obey requires learning to respond to one's parents with "modesty [and] humility,"[207] not because parents are good in themselves, but because of the call given to them by God. When a child honors her parents, she is honoring God. When she dishonors her parents, she dishonors God.

In my first parish, we had weekly children's messages in our chancel during the Divine Service. I was the one who typically sat with the children to teach them, but on occasion we had elders do it. Whenever the elder conducted them, I sat in my chair to the side of the pulpit with a great front row seat. The children sat about twenty feet in front of me in full view.

The elder welcomed the children as was customary and then started off with a question: "Boys and girls, *where is God?*" There were several children there that morning, and it was as if they had been prepped by someone before they came up. All of them, in concert, turned ninety degrees toward me and looked at me, the pastor. In their little minds, God was sitting just over there, not far from them. I laughed, but I knew the significance of what had just happened.

Parents—like pastors—represent God to their children. Therefore, parents are to be not only obeyed but honored as well. Luther said: "We must, therefore, impress this truth upon the young [Deuteronomy 6:7] that they should think of their parents as standing in God's place."[208] Such a view is assuredly not easy for children as they get older. They, too, live in the same household, and they eventually figure out that their parents also fall short of the glory of God (Romans 3:23). On this account, children are tempted to think, "Your parents don't *deserve* your obedience and honor."

---

205   Large Catechism I 103.
206   Large Catechism I 105.
207   Large Catechism I 106.
208   Large Catechism I 108. Brackets in original.

The temptation, however, is entirely misleading. What the parents may be in their persons is completely beside the point. We honor our parents not because they are good enough in our eyes but on account of God's Word and God's *call*. And in this way—by the way—the child also begins to learn how he or she will also know a successful marriage someday, as the same holds true toward our spouse.

The Call Is for Life

While it is true that our horizontal calls are prioritized by God so that, for example, while parents are a child's chief neighbors *before* marriage, that all changes after marriage. After marriage, the spouse is put before any other neighbor, including parents. Furthermore, when children come, then parents drop one more notch on the priority list, though their position in our lives is ever radiant.

Nevertheless, the Fourth Commandment is always in effect. Its importance is demonstrated by our Lord Jesus Christ. At the glorious moment of the incarnation, when God took on flesh and became completely God and completely man, He was (and still is) God in the flesh, the Almighty.

And at the same time, He kept the Fourth Commandment. Luke 2 records the young Jesus at twelve years old returning to the temple in Jerusalem without the knowledge of His parents. Joseph and Mary were worried sick when they discovered that Jesus was not with their company traveling back to Nazareth from Jerusalem. Where had He gone? Was He all right? This is when parents start producing more grey hairs.

They found their son in the temple, and Mary said, "Son, why have You treated us so? Behold, Your father and I have been searching for You in great distress" (Luke 2:48). The Lord replied with all truth and purity: "Why were you looking for Me? Did you not know that I must be in My Father's house?" (Luke 2:49). In connection to the present consideration, it is what we have at verse 51 that is especially pertinent: "And [Jesus] went down with [His parents] and came to Nazareth and was submissive to them."

Arthur Just states simply, "He let himself be placed in the proper divine ordering of the family."[209] By doing so, our Lord was living out the call given to all children so that God's righteous requirement to obey and honor parents would be fulfilled. This, too, is part and parcel of our salvation in Christ. But see the enormity of the call: almighty God submitted to His parents!

Christ kept the Fourth Commandment during His entire life on earth. When hanging from the cross, He spoke one of His last seven sayings to Mary and to His disciple John. The apostle recorded, "When Jesus saw His mother and the disciple whom He loved standing nearby, He said to His mother, 'Woman, behold, your son!' Then He said to the disciple, 'Behold, your mother!' And from that hour the disciple took her to his own home" (John 19:26–27). Even while dying, Jesus was honoring His mother and fulfilling the call of the Fourth Commandment.

Luther makes it clear that the child's call is for life:

> Learn, therefore, what is the honor towards parents that this commandment requires. (a) They must be held in distinction and esteem above all things, as the most precious treasure on earth. (b) In our words we must speak modestly toward them [Proverbs 15:1]. Do not address them roughly, haughtily, and defiantly. But yield to them and be silent, even though they go too far. (c) We must show them such honor also by works, that is, with our body and possessions. We must serve them, help them, and provide for them when they are old, sick, infirm, or poor. We must do all this not only gladly, but with humility and reverence, as doing it before God [Ephesians 6:6–7]. For the child who knows how to regard parents in his heart will not allow them to do without or hunger, but will place them above him and at his side and will share with them whatever he has and possesses.[210]

---

209   Arthur A. Just Jr., *Luke 1:1–9:50*, Concordia Commentary (St. Louis: Concordia Publishing House, 1996), 128.

210   Large Catechism I 109–11.

When my dad was in his twilight and frail, the Lord blessed me with some golden opportunities to love him and honor him. Once, he needed assistance to navigate into the shower. My instant response was "No problem!" I was in my forties, his youngest son, and his biggest son at six foot five and 280 pounds. I wrapped my arms around my dad's torso and took him step-by-step into the shower. There was just one problem: the only way I could get him in was for me to go in first. So, that's what I did. What made it interesting though was that the shower was already running, and I was still in my pajamas. I held him as we laughed together.

On another occasion, I needed to help my dad get into my van. I got him up from his wheelchair and we were off and running. My gentle hoist got him to the edge of the seat, but all at once, he started sliding off. Instinctively, I did what was necessary to cushion his slide onto the floorboard of my van. I caught him just in time, wrapping my arms around him and holding him as we went down together. There we were on the floor, holding each other and laughing, a moment I wouldn't trade for the world.

I got to honor him, and I was greatly blessed.

Children Who Shine into the Other Two Estates

When Luther wrote the meaning of the Fourth Commandment, he did not limit the obedience and honor children owe only to parents but also to "masters," or as other translations present it, "authorities." That is, the Fourth Commandment is the basis for good citizens who honor and most constructively work with the other estates, the church and state. These citizens understand that authority is a gift from God. When Hagar thought that she and her son would die in the desert, she was rescued and enlivened by the preincarnate Christ and said, "'You are a God of seeing,' for she said, 'Truly here I have seen Him who looks after me'" (Genesis 16:13). God establishes authorities that we may be seen and looked after.

Parents who do what God calls them to do are inherently influenced and inspired by the church estate when the church is faithful to God's Word. Thus, the instruction they provide inculcates the need to continue to submit to authority and not fall prey to the excessive individualism of our time when people desire to be their own authorities, causing the destabilization of culture.

When children see God in their parents, then they are much more apt to seek God beyond their parents. Such parents and children who know the gift of authorities who protect, serve, nurture, and guide will be drawn to the church estate to know the prime authority who showers His people with love and mercy in Christ. In the church estate, children see the good that can come from godly authority, and this experience and insight enables them to become fortifying members of culture.

But when parents disregard the importance of their own authority and responsibility, it indicates that they do not value the authority represented by the church estate. Chances are that worshiping in church and catechesis of the family will not be a priority, and the children will learn from their parents to discard the church. This in turn will contribute to the dissipation of the family's conscience, and the ability to discern right from wrong will fade.

When family and church no longer teach Christ's light also shining through authority, then the so-called authority of the state will become a vacuum for believing all things and practicing all things. In other words, it will ultimately represent believing in nothing and practicing whatever current ideology is here today and gone tomorrow.

When I asked Michael Salemink about the family's relationship to the state, he described a heart/family and soul/church that can train the mind/state to see the inestimably valuable need for the three states to work together:

> I would say the state only has any role or authority as it is delegated by the family. Remembering that helps understand the limit. The government has a claim on me because God and my parents have delegated some of their claim. Likewise, I have the responsibility to tell the government where its limits are because I am the primary agent of God to my family. It means, then, that we have certain responsibilities to my neighbor because we share life with them and not only with our

family. So, civic action is a means by which we love both our neighbor and our family, because it is one of the ways that we serve the government that acts as an agent on behalf when I can't do it myself.[211]

There are other indispensable members of the family and church who are the light of the world, who share life with us, and who are as much family as anyone else. We will now consider Christ's light through those who are single like Jesus was.

211   Salemink, interview.

CHAPTER 7 DISCUSSION GUIDE

Christ's Light through Parents and Children

UNCOVER INFORMATION

1. According to Ephesians 6:4, what are fathers to avoid and what are they to do?

2. How does Salemink describe the father and the family's devotional life?

3. What is the cross of the parent?

4. Who are those cared for in Matthew 25 according to Luther?

5. How are children commanded to treat their parents?

DISCOVER MEANING

1. How does the father exercise his headship according to Winger?

2. According to Luther, the responsibility to teach children the faith is undeniably important, so what should be done with a child who is unwilling to learn?

3. In referring to Christian fathers, the author writes, "He is their first pastor." What do you think this means?

4. If the Christian parent's children are those served in Matthew 25, how important are they to God?

5. How do children conduct themselves when they honor their parents?

Explore Implications

1. What does "bring them up" mean? What does it imply for the proper treatment of children?

2. Describe the enormity and blessing of fatherhood.

3. What does it say about a parent who suffers with the child when his or her child suffers?

4. If Luther is correct about Matthew 25, will the faithful parent be enabled by God to serve in this way?

5. Since parents represent God to their children, who are children really honoring when they honor their parents?

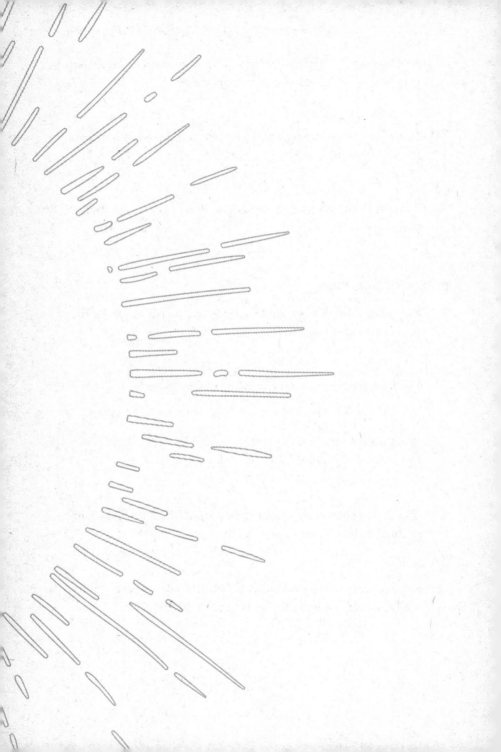

CHRIST'S LIGHT THROUGH SINGLENESS

Not a Subcategory, but a Whole Family

We've already referred to marriage as the highest call within the family, but there is another call to the Christian who is single that mirrors the supreme call, not any horizontal call, but the vertical call: it is the call to be a Christian who lives in singleness. Such a Christian can shine the vertical call of God even more brightly than a married Christian can. At the same time, for single people in Christ, singleness has everything to do with family.

St. Matthew records an invaluable lesson that should be considered for any proper understanding of Christian singleness:

> While He was still speaking to the people, behold, His mother and His brothers stood outside, asking to speak to Him. But He replied to the man who told Him, "Who is My mother, and who are My brothers?" And stretching out His hand toward His disciples, He said, "Here are My mother and My brothers! For whoever does the will of My Father in heaven is My brother and sister and mother." (Matthew 12:46–50)

Jeffrey Gibbs lays out the reality Jesus taught here: "Of all human relationships, none can be as important as the family relationship to Jesus that comes through being his disciple."[212] When Jesus spoke

---

212   Jeffrey A. Gibbs, *Matthew 11:2–20:34*, Concordia Commentary (St. Louis: Concordia Publishing House, 2010), 656.

these words, He probably shocked many of the people listening in, and even today some Christians might not want to admit that these words challenge them, especially when they might be apt to idolize marriage.

In no way was the Lord Jesus diminishing the holiness of marriage and the Fourth Commandment. Still, to be His disciple was "to [Jesus] of a higher order and greater priority than the familial relationships established by God in the creation of marriage and family. . . . Jesus' disciples are *his* family, and he is their brother in the most important and profound sense possible."[213]

No, we are not making a one-for-one correspondence between singleness and faithful discipleship, but for any unmarried Christian who is serious about discipleship to Christ—who "does the will of My Father in heaven" (Matthew 12:50)—this Christian is not "single" but belongs to the greatest family on earth.

Singleness for the Right Reasons

We are not, of course, condoning living together apart from marriage—which is an attempt to have your cake and eat it too. Such a way of life essentially says that you're married and not married at the same time, which is, of course, impossible. By doing so, a couple dishonors the Lord, as He has established that sexual consummation is an expression of what God does in joining a man and a woman together in holy marriage. Living together, yes even in the twenty-first century, is still a violation of the Sixth Commandment.

It is also important that the Christian living in singleness does not overdesire or underdesire marriage, as either of these will have a negative impact on living in singleness.[214] At the end of the day, either being married or not is a good place for a Christian to be when she is faithful in her vertical call as a baptized child of God. "We should be neither overly elated by getting married nor overly disappointed by not being so—because Christ is the only spouse that can truly fulfill us and God's family the only family that will truly embrace and satisfy us."[215]

---

213 Gibbs, *Matthew 11:2–20:34*, 657.

214 Keller and Keller, *The Meaning of Marriage*, 192.

215 Keller and Keller, *The Meaning of Marriage*, 194.

Marriage itself, in fact, points to the real marriage and family more important than anything: our marriage to Jesus Christ and our family the Holy Church.[216]

Singleness Testifies That Christ Is First

The Lord will not permit putting our earthly families on a pedestal. Jesus said, "Do not think that I have come to bring peace to the earth, I have not come to bring peace, but a sword. For I have come to set a man against his father, and a daughter against her mother, and a daughter-in-law against her mother-in-law. And a person's enemies will be those of his own household" (Matthew 10:34–36). Gibbs reminds, "Even the family, the closest and most fundamental unit in human existence, will be affected [because some believe, and others do not]."[217]

Why mention this? Because every horizontal call is a gift from God. And every gift from God—as St. Paul presents gifts in 1 Corinthians 12:7—is "the manifestation of the Spirit for the common good." Keller reminds us that the call to singleness is also a gift for building others up.[218] And the gift of singleness is one which St. Paul says grants the unmarried Christian the opportunity to be free from the anxieties attached to marriage so that he may be wholly able to be anxious for how to please the Lord (1 Corinthians 7:32–35). So, the potential division within the earthly family as is recorded in Matthew 10:34–36 is a reminder that we have a greater loyalty to a family that will last forever. This reminder is something that the Christian living in singleness can keep before the church.

Singleness for the Kingdom of Heaven

In Matthew 19:12, the Lord Jesus taught, *"And there are eunuchs who have made themselves eunuchs for the sake of the kingdom of heaven."* This does not mean in this case that these men have been castrated but rather points to a sacred commitment to God. Gibbs explains, "God has given to some men (and by extension, we could also say some women)

---

216   Keller and Keller, *The Meaning of Marriage*, 198.

217   Gibbs, *Matthew 1:1–11:1*, 539.

218   Keller and Keller, *The Meaning of Marriage*, 207.

the ability to accept a different calling and to set aside the gift of marriage in order to devote themselves more fully to the purposes of God, who is at work in Jesus [for His reign in the world]."[219]

Peters recognizes that the higher view of family permits a kind of "reordering" from a Christian perspective: "The newly instituted *Familia Dei*, which treated being taken into God's household as being in a brotherly relationship with Jesus, dissolves the primary sacral bond of blood relationships with earth and opens at the same time the radical possibility that one would even make oneself a eunuch for the sake of the kingdom of heaven."[220]

That is, a Christian may be bold to firmly hold to the fact that to choose celibacy for the kingdom of God is a holy estate while affirming the family of God as the primary family. Furthermore, Gibbs points out that "for the sake of the kingdom of heaven" is not the equivalent of a holy order, such as a man or woman entering the pastoral ministry, deaconate, or missionary field.[221] "One can think of several motivations that would fit into the general category 'on account of the reign of heaven,' and the celibate life of laypersons is no less God-pleasing than that of those called to full-time service in the church."[222]

Singleness and the Cross

Devout Christians who live in singleness must often endure caricatures that come with being single. Shamefully, being the object of people putting the worst construction on things can even come from within the church.

While it is true that people dominated by their sinful nature will use singleness as an opportunity to invest more in the gods of this age like success, money, sex, and power, it is imperative that within the church we remember St. Paul's directive: "But in humility count others more significant than yourselves" (Philippians 2:3). The church should praise God for the *gift* of brothers and sisters in Christ who live in singleness.

---

219 Gibbs, *Matthew 11:2–20:34*, 955.
220 Peters, *Commentary on Luther's Catechisms*, 117.
221 Gibbs, *Matthew 11:2–20:34*, 955.
222 Gibbs, *Matthew 11:2–20:34*, 955.

Even when a Christian living in singleness, however, can cover others with grace when they don't understand, there is still a heavier cross that often comes with singleness: the desire for sexual intimacy in a relationship. We must be careful in our handling of 1 Corinthians 7:2, 9. At verse 2, St. Paul says, "Because of the temptation to sexual immorality [a person should marry]." In addition, at verse 9, he wrote, "But if they cannot exercise self-control, they should marry. For it is better to marry than to burn with passion."

There are some things, however, to keep in perspective. First, we can't ignore the words in the *Agenda* for holy matrimony, "Therefore, all persons who marry shall take a spouse in holiness and honor, not in the passion of lust, for God has not called us to impurity but in holiness."[223] While marriage is to also satisfy sexual desire, it is not to be viewed *merely* as the answer for curbing passion. At this juncture, we have entered a tension.

Second, St. Paul is clear about the *qualifier* at 1 Corinthians 7:9: "But if they cannot exercise self-control," and this is an important qualification to say the least. Inherent in the biblical instruction is the possibility that some unmarried Christians *could* maintain self-control. That is, the Lord can grant this ability (or better said, *gift*) where and when He pleases. And certainly, if a Christian has this gift, nothing prohibits her from getting married, but clearly she is free not to.

Third, St. Paul is dealing with the most serious immoral possibilities when he wrote, "Better to marry than to burn with passion." Gregory J. Lockwood provides insight: "The apostle insists, however, that an exception must be made to his advice that widowers and widows remain as he does. If they lack self-control and are tempted to visit prostitutes (cf. 7:2) or indulge in extramarital affairs, then the remedy is that they must marry."[224]

Thus, now we clearly see the possibility of a real cross: that while a Christian may serve in his call to be single, he might find himself lacking self-control to maintain this calling. To constantly crucify the

---

223   *Lutheran Service Book: Agenda* (St. Louis: Concordia Publishing House, 2006), 65.
224   Gregory J. Lockwood, *1 Corinthians*, Concordia Commentary (St. Louis: Concordia Publishing House, 2000), 236.

desire of the flesh, especially when it is in line with our created instinct for physical, emotional, and spiritual companionship, is to know the fight we described above.[225]

What does a Christian living in singleness do when this is the case? There is no question that the Christian should be intentional in her prayers both that the Lord would grant a godly spouse and also that God's will be done. However, it is equally as important that she pray to the Lord to grant help in the face of burning passion. This was put forth above, but it is worth repeating here for our current discussion:

> If pain or sickness afflicts you, consider how paltry this is in comparison with the thorny crown and the nails of Christ. If you are obliged to do or to refrain from doing things against your wishes, ponder how Christ was bound and captured and led hither and yon. If you are beset by pride, see how your Lord was mocked and ridiculed along with criminals. If unchastity and lust assail you, remember how ruthlessly Christ's tender flesh was scourged, pierced, and beaten. If hatred, envy, and vindictiveness beset you, recall that Christ, who indeed had more reason to avenge himself, interceded with tears and cries for you and for all his enemies. If sadness or any adversity, physical or spiritual, distresses you, strengthen your heart and say, "Well, why should I not be willing to bear a little grief, when agonies and fears caused my Lord to sweat blood in the Garden of Gethsemane?"[226]

It is critical to remember that when Christ bore our sin, He didn't bear only certain sin but *all of them*. Notice the line in the middle in the above quotation from Luther: *"If unchastity and lust assail you, remember how ruthlessly Christ's tender flesh was scourged, pierced, and beaten."* There is no sin that our Lord did not address in His life and death for us.

---

225   Chapter 3.
226   AE 42:13–14.

But there is still one more vital facet that we mustn't forget: we need the Body of Christ, our pastors, and our fellow Christians. We should never face our fights, burdens, and crosses alone. We must find confidants who will not condemn us but who will encourage us and be there for us in a trustworthy manner. The investment in friendships of the same feather can go a long way in standing alongside the Christian who is both single and seeking a future spouse. We are not in the fight alone, and we don't have to bear our crosses by ourselves.

Singleness That Counters Excessive Individualism

If there are any people who qualify in our twenty-first-century culture as having full freedom to live for themselves, then assuredly single adults are the pool to draw from. From the world's perspective, no one can blame such a person who goes all out to do what he wants to do. Isn't this the dream? Isn't this what life's all about? We know how sin, the world, and the devil would answer.

No one, but no one, can stand face to face with these enemies of the Spirit better than the Christian living in singleness, who can answer "No!" The Christian living in singleness can be warrior against extreme individualism.

Such a position assuredly will seem both uncanny and untenable to the current culture. The single Christian, however, may present herself to the culture as a walking paradox: as one possessing all freedom while choosing to make herself a servant to all.[227]

That is to say, the Christian living in singleness represents the light of Christ the world needs desperately to shine for its darkness. Such a light shines upon the family estate announcing, "Do not forget your greater family, Christians; you are, above all, children of God, brothers and sisters of Jesus Christ, and heirs of an eternal family." Such Christians speak to the family estate so that those who are married do not turn their families into earthly idols.

Such Christians also shine upon the church estate: they remind us that the church is not an appendage in the culture but the place where

---

227   Reminiscent of Luther's *Treatise on Christian Liberty* (AE 31:344): (1) "A Christian is a perfectly free lord of all, subject to none." (2) "A Christian is a perfectly dutiful servant of all, subject to all."

the love of Christ gives us strength to face those battles that seem impossible. It is often the Christian who lives in singleness who can inspire a Christian congregation to remember that we really do *need* each other as we gather for God's grace and then serve each other to live in that grace.

And finally, such Christians shine upon the state, a state in a culture that is increasingly promoting excessive individualism. Christians living in singleness can say, "I am single and free, but if we forget that we are here to serve others, then we will destroy ourselves, because living for oneself is the cancer of the heart and soul of our lives." Therefore, the estate that is analogous to the human mind must fill itself with thoughts of virtue so that the state does not destroy itself.

Great Gifts to the Church

I've had the privilege over the years to serve many Christians living in singleness. Two of them I've served more recently. They are middle-aged adults, one a sister in Christ and the other a brother in Christ. If one were considering candidates for marriage, you would have a hard time finding better future spouses than either of them. They are outstanding Christians and gifted in every aspect of personality, appearance, and their respective careers; they have lots of friends, are fun to be around, and have devout faith. And both show confidence and peace in their call to singleness.

My sister in Christ has arranged her garage in her townhome community so that when she has a little leisure time, it is set up for her not only to enjoy a good read but also to be intentional about shining the light of Christ to her neighbors. I brought the Sacrament to her one day, and we sat in her garage because it was a beautiful day. What I witnessed that day made my heart rejoice.

In the hour I was there, I couldn't believe how many of her neighbors walked by. Some were returning from taking their kids out, others walking their dogs, or another taking out some trash. My parishioner greeted all of them by name and, in most of the cases, introduced me to them. It was abundantly clear that these people knew her well and treated her like a beam of sunlight. Her love for Jesus and for people overflows. I saw the definition of a good neighbor that day and why she knows peace and joy as a Christian living in singleness. She's joyful and does not hesitate to live her faith, offering words that uplift and a helpful hand to anyone in need. Jesus lives in that garage.

My brother in Christ works as an instructor of theology at a Christian high school. The reason I mention this is that when teachers are always presenting and talking about a given subject—any subject—it is understandable when they need to step back and take breaks from their field. But for this man of faith, when he talks about the saving faith, one hears not just what is on his mind but what is in his heart and soul. And he does it so well that young adults respond to him. He is impressively social and one of the friendliest men I know. As he is a member of my congregation, he invited an outstanding colleague to church who kept coming back. I ended up catechizing and confirming her. This is an example of how my parishioner seems to shine Christ's light 24/7.

I reached out to him when I was thinking about starting an audio and visual podcast for yet another way of reaching out with the saving Gospel of Jesus Christ. I knew he had some experience with podcasts, so I sought his advice. He was nothing but helpful, but not only helpful, he was wonderfully enthusiastic and encouraging as he supplied me with confidence to take the next step.

It seemed natural for me to ask him if he would think about serving alongside me. He agreed and suggested one of his theology co-instructors join us. Then, we were blessed with a fourth man, who is our producer, one of the elders in our congregation. The four of us are now off and running to the glory of God. In the meantime, I cannot say enough about my brother in Christ. He is living proof that Christians living in singleness are gifts from God.

God's gifts that shine the light of Christ are also specifically within the estate of the church, and the callings we find there are invaluable to our lives. It is time to consider them.

CHAPTER 8 DISCUSSION GUIDE

Christ's Light through Singleness

UNCOVER INFORMATION

1. Singleness mirrors the supreme call, not any horizontal call, but the _____ call from God.

2. Why is living together apart from marriage a sin?

3. How does Matthew 10:34–36 prevent us from putting family on a pedestal?

4. How might singleness be a cross for a Christian?

5. What may Christian singleness constructively counter in our culture?

DISCOVER MEANING

1. Why is the most important family relationship to Jesus being His disciple?

2. What do we mean by saying that a single Christian should not overdesire or underdesire marriage?

3. How does 1 Corinthians 12:7 inform us about singleness? How can this be true?

4. What is the *qualifier* in 1 Corinthians 7:9 that teaches us that it is better to marry?

5. What do we mean that the Christian single can be "a walking paradox" in a good way?

Explore Implications

1. How can we say that the Christian single belongs to the greatest family on earth?

2. Why do we say that Christ is the only spouse that can truly fulfill us?

3. How might a single Christian teach all Christians about the importance of the family of God?

4. Why would it be helpful to consider Christ's flesh on the cross when tempted by sexual desire?

5. How can the single Christian be a great gift to the church by his or her example to other Christians?

PART IV

Christ's Light through Church Callings

	## Church Vocations
Pastor	
Priesthood	
Congregation to the World	

CHRIST'S LIGHT THROUGH PASTORS AND PRIESTHOOD

The Church: Salt, Light, and Conscience

Before the light of the world, Jesus, called His Christians "the light of the world" (Matthew 5:14), He called them something else first:

> You are the salt of the earth, but if salt has lost its taste, how shall its saltiness be restored? It is no longer good for anything except to be thrown out and trampled under people's feet. (Matthew 5:13)

Gibbs sees the construction of verse 13, "salt *of the earth*," as "that which salts the earth."[228] The wording helps set up the light metaphor referring to Christians: "You are that which gives light to the world."[229] "The impact of the salt and light metaphors has to do with the beneficial effect Jesus' disciples have on the *world* in which they live as disciples."[230] Christians benefit the world by salting the earth and giving light to the world.

In the history of the Old Testament and of the Christian Church, both the use of salt and the interpretation of salt in its various contexts have resulted in many different traditions and meanings. Here in

---

228   Gibbs, *Matthew 1:1–11:1*, 257.

229   Gibbs, *Matthew 1:1–11:1*, 257. This is the translation offered by Dr. Gibbs.

230   Gibbs, *Matthew 1:1–11:1*, 257.

Matthew 5, however, our Lord elaborates on the Christian's status as salt and light by teaching on very practical issues of life: anger, judgment, lust, adultery, divorce, taking oaths, retaliation, and love for enemies. He is speaking about the moral condition of people, and while Christianity is not *about* morality, true faith in the Savior Christ will have a great *impact upon a person's morality*, which—when that person is in Christ—gives evidence of a "healthy tree" (Matthew 7:17) and of "a wise man who built his house on the rock" (Matthew 7:24).

With this context, Lenski saw the primary use of salt in the context here in Matthew 5:13:

> All that Christ has in mind with the figure of salt is that His disciples check the moral corruption of the world, so that it does not quickly perish in its own moral rottenness. . . . This is due to the fact that Christ and the kingdom dwell in [Christians], changing our inward nature and working not only in us but also through us in blessing for the whole earth.[231]

Recall that in chapter 5 we made the case that, in relation to the other estates, the Christian Church is like the conscience of the family, having direct impact upon the state. And what does the conscience do? It salts the world, making people aware of what is good and what is evil, what is right and what is wrong. And as the estate of the church points to Jesus Christ, both the family and the state will know exactly the antithesis against all that is corrupting.

The First Priority: God's Community of Lights

We can talk all day about the church's influence upon the world, but if the church is not healthy within herself, then the church estate will have little impact beyond its walls. This is not to say that Christian congregations are expected to be perfect. Not even close, but they are able to experience exactly what makes the light of the church so luminous: it is a community of people who know how God deals with hearts described in Scripture as "deceitful . . . and desperately sick" (Jeremiah

---

231   Lenski, *St. Matthew's Gospel*, 199.

17:9). It is a community of sinners who have received Christ's love and mercy, living in a state of grace. They are people transformed into a new community—not a community of judgment but one of healing, and not just among themselves but for the world they go out to in their holy family and state vocations.

But if they will go out this way, then they must know that first, they have vocations toward one another within the church. These congregational vocations are essential, and we cannot reduce them to mere volunteerism. St. Paul taught this in Galatians:

> And let us not grow weary of doing good, for in due season we will reap, if we do not give up. So then, as we have opportunity, let us do good to everyone, and especially to those who are of the household of faith. (Galatians 6:9–10)

God's love in Christ is universal and is for all, regardless as to where they are in life, and regardless as to whether they have saving faith or not. At the same time, St. Paul presents a priority for Christians: "Let us do good to everyone, *and especially to those who are of the household of faith.*" Lenski again, "All their spiritual needs are seen and felt by us in the most immediate way. They and we are joined together with them as we are with no others."[232]

It is imperative, therefore, that the light of Christ radiating from the church estate begin with a robust sharing of Christ's light to fellow Christians in the local faith community, the congregation. This is the context for callings often taken for granted but which the church could not function without. Let us consider the backdrop for the holy vocations within the church where Christians gather for Divine Service, where the Lord is worshiped in spirit and in truth (John 4:24). It is the holy sanctuary itself where Christ's light radiates for God's people, upon them, within them, and through them.

---

232   Lenski, *St. Paul's Epistles*, 311.

Christ's Light in the Holy Place, the Sanctuary

God's people gather in the *nave* where they worship, the word taken from the Latin for "ship." The nave reminds us of how God saved Noah and his family in the ark. The nave symbolizes that we are going through the storm of life in the world where sin has entered but we find refuge and sanctuary in the holy place where Christ meets us through His Word and Sacrament to save us from darkness.

The nave goes forward to connect to the higher chancel, where the pastor(s) and assistants in the Divine Service serve God's people, and of course, the chancel leads up to the altar (the high place) from which the light of the world—Jesus Christ—sheds His light upon His people.

The two candles on the altar represent the two natures of Christ, and from this altar we are given His very body and blood in, with, and under the bread and wine in connection to the consecration, distribution, and reception of the Holy Sacrament. Through the Eucharist, the light of the world enters His people.

There are many things that the seven candles in a candelabra may represent (like the seven gifts of the Holy Spirit),[233] but they also represent the seven churches in the Book of Revelation 1:4, 12–13.[234] Thus, the candelabra also represent that Jesus—the light of the world—is in the midst of His Church, where His light overflows. In this way, the acolytes in the Divine Service are the first proclaimers of God with us. Though they do not speak a word, they light the candles that tell us Christ comes into our midst and that His light shines upon us.

Next to the baptismal font is the paschal candle, which represents our new lives in Christ, who is the resurrection and the life (John 11:25). The word *paschal* takes us back to the Old Testament Passover, when God's people were passed over by death through the blood of the lamb. In Holy Baptism, we are covered by the blood of the Lamb and pass

---

233 Friedrich Rest, *Our Christian Symbols* (Cleveland, OH: The Pilgrim Press, 1954), 13. Here, Rest lists, "Wisdom, understanding, counsel, might, knowledge, piety, and fear of the Lord, six are mentioned in Isaiah 11:2. Piety was added later. The list from Revelation 5:12 consists of power, wealth, wisdom, might, honor, glory, and blessing."

234 Some candelabra may have less than seven candles. Their numerology will still be rich in biblical meaning.

from death to life (John 5:24). Light is shining every time someone is baptized into Christ.

There is also in the chancel and altar area an eternal flame, which represents all the saints in heaven. When we gather in Divine Service, we are united with all Christians of all time and worship "with angels and archangels and with all the company of heaven."[235]

Sometimes congregations will have torches on either side of the pulpit, which may also be carried in procession for the Holy Gospel to be read in the midst of God's people in the nave. This is yet another way that Christ's light enters His people: His Word traveling from the mouth of the pastor into the ears, hearts, and minds of the Christians receiving it.

The people of God in this holy house are bathed in the light of Christ to the extent that they are transformed: they *themselves* become light. They are indeed extensions of Christ. These are the lights of Christ in the pews, and referring to these, Jesus said, "You are the light of the world" (Matthew 5:14).

Light is everywhere in the holy place, the sacred sanctuary where Christ meets us sacramentally. And it is where the call to be a Christian takes place. The word *church* itself means "the called-out ones." St. Peter wrote, "But you are a chosen race, a royal priesthood, a holy nation, a people for His own possession, that you may proclaim the excellencies of Him who called you out of darkness into His marvelous light" (1 Peter 2:9).

To be God's "own possession" is like being God's "peculiar treasure" (Exodus 19:5 KJV); "a special people unto Himself" (Deuteronomy 7:6 KJV); made to be God's very own like jewels (Malachi 3:17 KJV); a select people (Titus 2:14 KJV); and bought with a price (1 Corinthians 6:20).[236] These "proclaim [God's] excellencies . . . who called [Christians] out of darkness into [God's] marvelous light." This Scripture restates 1 Peter 2:5: "You yourselves like living stones are being built up as a spiritual house,

---

235   The Proper Preface in the Divine Service (*LSB*, p. 208).

236   R. C. H. Lenski, *The Interpretation of I and II Peter, the Three Epistles of John, and the Epistle of Jude* (Minneapolis: Augsburg, 1966), 102.

to be a holy priesthood, to offer spiritual sacrifices acceptable to God through Jesus Christ."[237]

Christians are now equipped by Christ to shine "the light of truth, life, [and] blessedness which are found in the kingdom of grace."[238] And this light is over and above "darkness," which is "the state of the world under the prince of darkness, the state of blindness, lifelessness, [and] death, in which the world still lies."[239]

Christians gather in Christ's sanctuary and holy place of light and they become and are sustained as light. But once again, before the urgent call to shine in the world, they are also called to shine within the church itself since the church is filled with sinners who continue to desperately need the light of Christ. If the members of the church do not serve each other, then their light to the world will be dimmed and therefore less effective.

The Pastor Gives Light

When the pastor faithfully preaches the Word of Christ, something remarkable happens. The power of this event, however, has nothing to do with the pastor, who in himself is only a poor sinner, but has everything to do with the office from which he preaches and the Word preached, both of which belong to Christ.

Timothy Seals described the significance of preaching: "This is truly a miracle. Luther valued the preached word; the authentic Word of God is the Word of God in worship because Christ is there, and when that Word is preached, Christ is speaking."[240] As he prepares, he also described his own practice in coming forward to preach. He prays to God, "Get me out of the way, my ego out of the way, or [put it] . . . in its proper place."[241]

Luther taught how serious this call to preach is. He wrote, "I have the commission and charge, as a preacher and a doctor, to see to it that

---

237   Lenski, *I and II Peter*, 103.

238   Lenski, *I and II Peter*, 103–4.

239   Lenski, *I and II Peter*, 103.

240   Timothy Seals, live interview by author, Zoom video call, September 6, 2022.

241   Seals, interview.

no one is misled, so that I may give account of it at the Last Judgement (Heb 13:17)."[242] He also clarified about whose office the preaching office is: "I have often said that the office of preaching is not our office but God's. But whatever is God's, that we do not do ourselves; but He does it Himself, through the Word and the office, as His own gift and business."[243] In this preaching, the pastor serves but, at the same time, cannot tolerate whatever is against Christ and His Word. Luther says, "But to God's enemies I must also be an enemy, lest I join forces with them against God."[244]

Such pastors, according to the Large Catechism, are spiritual fathers.[245] Only these are called such "who govern and guide us by God's Word."[246] But while pastors are worthy of double honor (1 Timothy 5:17–18) in the church, to the rest of world they are "like . . . filth . . . and everybody's refuse and footrag."[247]

But within the church, the pastors give light to God's people. Luther elaborated on Matthew 5:14–15, where the Lord calls us light, and said, "The office of the ministry and the Word of God are supposed to shine forth like the sun."[248] Luther says, "They are called a 'light of the world' and are to be one; that is, they are to instruct souls and guide them to eternal life."[249]

Luther included the laity as emitting Christ's light by also explaining that pastors shine through their teaching "by which . . . others . . . believe."[250] And these follow with good works, "which shine, too, but only insofar as they are ignited and sustained by faith."[251] But consider

---

242   AE 21:44.

243   AE 21:119.

244   AE 21:121–22.

245   Large Catechism I 158.

246   Large Catechism I 158.

247   Large Catechism I 160. From the world's perspective, which admires power and prestige. St. Paul refers to the apostles this way from the world's point of view (1 Corinthians 4:13).

248   AE 21:8.

249   AE 21:61.

250   AE 21:65.

251   AE 21:66.

what all of this implies: the light of Christ begins with the office of the ministry, which gives that light to God's people.

For this reason, pastors pay for this office of light. Pastor Seals describes the cost: "And when [the pastor is] connected to the light of God, [the pastor] is going to . . . beam, it will show, and it will bring persecution because [sin, the world, and the demonic] see the light and they will come after you, because that's what they do."[252]

The Pastor Needs Light

Elsewhere I wrote about the great need for pastors themselves to receive care—especially private confession and absolution—from other pastors. Certainly some of this care can come from the people of the church itself, but the need of the pastor for light is real:

> A seemingly endless list of demands invites an overwhelming sense of failure to seep into the pastor's soul. Endless expectations and demands may also make the ministry a *lonely* vocation in which the pastor feels spiritually and emotionally starved.[253]

A Pastor Sustained by His Own Congregation

I had developed the unfortunate habit of working twice as hard right before vacation so that I could actually go on vacation. Many years ago, I followed the pattern so that by the time Traci and I got the family packed in the van, I was exhausted.

Feeling this way justified the fact that when we stopped a few hours down the road for breakfast, I ordered a cup of coffee. It was so good I took a second, and a third, and a fourth. So, when we reembarked on our adventure up Highway 1 in California, I was now both tired and wired with caffeine. A few hours further up the highway, we stopped

---

252   Seals, interview.

253   *Confession and Absolution: A Report of the Commission on Theology and Church Relations* (St. Louis, MO: The Lutheran Church—Missouri Synod, 2018), 20–21.

for lunch, and I poured more concoctions into my system. We were off and running again before we knew it.

As I drove, however, I started to have a set of strange sensations. First, I started feeling heated and was looking for ways to cool myself, so I increased the fan, cracked the window a little, and even started fanning myself. But instead of feeling better, I started to become self-conscious about my breathing. To make things more interesting, I started feeling tingling in my fingers. I got off the freeway and turned onto a side road.

Traci asked me what was wrong, but I was too upset to answer. I opened my door immediately and sat sideways in the driver's seat with my feet outside on the ground, trying to get some fresh air, but I felt as though I was falling into a black whirlpool in my mind. I had never experienced anything like this before, and I thought I was dying. Traci took over the driving and got me to a hospital. All of this got our kids' attention as they wondered if I was going to be all right.

After some tests, the doctor told me I had experienced my first panic attack. Parishioners had told me about them, but I was now among the ranks of those who had been there and done that. However, I was exhausted as I lay in the hospital. And then something interesting happened. While I was now several hours from our home in south Orange County with my parish left in the capable hands of my co-pastor, I couldn't believe it when he walked in the hospital room. How had he gotten there, literally hours north of our parish? Did he suddenly sprout wings? Was he wearing a red cape? To this day, I have no idea how he arrived so quickly.

In addition, parishioners who had moved up north also came to visit me, but they took it a step further and insisted that I and my family come directly to their home upon my being released. When we arrived at their home, they went into overdrive to care for me. I got their best and most comfortable chair, some good food, a comfortable blanket, plenty of water, and the best care imaginable for myself and my family. Of course, Traci was by my side the entire time, as were my children, completely spoiling me. I was surrounded by a bunch of baptized saints. They prayed over me like the pastor had. *I was in the hands of God, and His light was upon me.*

Church Membership Is a Calling

Being a member of a local parish is not an avocation but a vocation; it is not a hobby but a calling. It isn't a side gig. And if it is considered as merely running in for a service and then running out as soon as the service ends, then we're missing something of its full significance.

Luther warned against something called *akadia*, which is apathy or satisfaction, and called it "a malignant, dangerous plague."[254] If a Christian has apathy toward the significance of belonging to a local congregation, then they are not only shooting themselves in the foot, but they are contributing to the deterioration of the church.

The local congregation needs her members. They are those called by God to first receive Christ's light and then to give it, beginning with their brothers and sisters in Christ, who are but poor sinners in serious need of encouragement and mutual service.

Gene Veith reminds us that "minimizing the ordinary local church is a great mistake. Christ is hidden in His Church on earth, and always has been."[255] And he explains why it is a mistake to take a reductionistic view of the church: "[In the book of Acts] we see that the church is a community of faith—not just a place to go to for an hour on Sunday morning, but a place where Christians are involved in each other's lives."[256] What is more, after Veith reminds us of the list of practical needs within the church, like covering its mortgage and conducting its tedious meetings, which are nevertheless vital, that the members through their "vocations in the secular arena [are] a big help for churches trying to navigate their way through the world."[257]

Brett Webb-Mitchell summarizes pedagogy from John Howard Yoder:

---

254   Large Catechism I 99.

255   Veith, *God at Work*, 115.

256   Veith, *God at Work*, 125.

257   Veith, *God at Work*, 131–32.

Whether it is the hand, the foot, the eye, or the ear in the body
of Christ, they all have the following characteristics in common
within the body of Christ: first, they are each vital and irre-
placeable; second, they possess and exercise their own duty
within the body of Christ with dignity; third, they can function fully only when they understand that they are bound to
the other members, and that bond is Christ; and fourth, each
member can be crippled through no fault of its own when
some other part of the body suffers.[258]

One of the main reasons people will cite for discontinuing their
active membership in the church is for crisis and conflict, but here
again, Webb-Mitchell provides excellent insight:

Rather than being a "bad" thing, crisis or conflict can lead
to our discovering the good we share in common in Christ's
body. To paraphrase what Jean Vanier often says, it is necessary
for a community to have individuals who are difficult to live
with: they make the community "interesting," and they may
also reveal the strengths and weaknesses in our churches. And
when such people are no longer there, mysteriously enough,
someone else will come to take their place. In truth, conflict
is often important in helping a community understand what
it means to live as a community. Conflict also unveils for all
to see and hear a community's convictions—as well as certain virtues Christians need to live together.[259]

In his inspirational and wise work *Life Together*, Dietrich Bonhoeffer
cut to the chase in reminding us why we need the church: "The more
isolated a person is, the more destructive will be the power of sin
over him, and the more deeply he becomes involved in it, the more
disastrous is his isolation. Sin wants to remain unknown. It shuns the

258   Brett P. Webb-Mitchell, *Christly Gestures: Learning to Be Members of the Body of Christ* (Grand Rapids, MI: William B. Eerdmans, 2003), 66.

259   Webb-Mitchell, *Christly Gestures*, 82–83.

light."[260] And Bonhoeffer does not underestimate the Word of Christ that comes from our fellow Christians: "[The Christian] needs his brother solely because of Jesus Christ. The Christ in his own heart is weaker than the Christ in the word of his brother; his own heart is uncertain, his brother's sure."[261]

This mutual ministry means that we have others to help bear our burdens. Dcs. Dr. Tiffany Manor, who is director of Life Ministry for The Lutheran Church—Missouri Synod, shared her insights about the call all Christians have toward one another:

> [In the sense of] Galatians 6:2, when you're bearing burdens with other people, when I'm with people and in the midst of their suffering or in their burdens or in their challenges, their load . . . specifically becomes lighter . . . [this] doesn't mean it's easy for me. I say it's a privilege. I say it's a joy. It is demanding, it is challenging, but they often will say things like . . . "I feel light now, I feel better now having talked with you." Being reminded of the faith in Christ, of God's Word [I read] . . . with them. So, in essence, it's what they are feeling because they had a servant of Christ alongside them.[262]

The Invaluable Light of the Church's Members

I took a big step from a congregation of about 250 members in Southern California to a congregation of about 850 in Texas. In my new call, I was now the senior pastor of a large staff. I arrived at this call in Texas at the ripe old age of 36.

The congregation was fantastic, and I loved my flock there. The labor in the ministry there was exceptional, as in it was easily exhausting. My predecessor, of whom I had tremendous respect, gave me a heads-up

---

260   Dietrich Bonhoeffer, *Life Together*, trans. John W. Doberstein (New York: Harper & Row, 1954), 112.

261   Bonhoeffer, *Life Together*, 23.

262   Tiffany Manor, live interview by author, St. Louis, MO: International Center, The Lutheran Church—Missouri Synod, June 16, 2022.

when I got started: "Al, this call is about a seven-year call." That was about how long he lasted, and he was an exceptionally gifted man of God.

He wasn't being pessimistic, but he wanted me to have a realistic sense of the workload, taking into consideration the demands for pastoral care, supervision of a large staff for the church and large preschool, and being the hub administrator in the center of the board of directors, a large board of elders, and of course the staff. My predecessor was basically right. I made it to about eight and a half years. I was blessed when I took my next call, because no one was asking me to leave. I loved my flock, and they loved me.

However, it was indeed a considerable change from my prior calls. The landscape was more complex. There was considerably more administration, and while I love the core service of the pastoral ministry, I am not exemplary in administrative leadership. One day, one of my fifteen elders suggested that we consider taking three of the elders with the most real-world experience in administration and form a "Pastor's Advisory Committee." We were off and running, and I met with my "PAC" on a regular basis.

These three men were amazing. While they honored me as their spiritual shepherd who fed their souls with the Word of God, it was like I had gone back to school as I received the tutelage of these servants of God. They had training and experience in high-level management, and their applied wisdom was off the charts.

What I quickly realized was that while the meetings were about administration specifically, they were making the pastoral ministry, the spiritual ministry, more efficient. They were making me stronger and the congregation stronger so that the ministry of Christ's Word and Sacrament was stronger. They made the light of Christ shine more brightly in our congregation.

This is why every single member in the congregation and even the weakest members are—again, as St. Paul says at 1 Corinthians 12:22—"indispensable" to the Body of Christ. The pastor and people of the church are lights. And when they share this light with one another, then they are in a better position to step outside the congregation and continue shining for Christ. To this endeavor we now turn.

CHAPTER 9 DISCUSSION GUIDE

Christ's Light through Pastors and Priesthood

UNCOVER INFORMATION

1. Besides the Lord calling Christians "the light of the world," what else does He call them?

2. What are Christians to be toward one another in the church?

3. What does *nave* mean? List some of the lights within it.

4. How does the pastor give light to God's people?

5. How is being a church member a calling?

DISCOVER MEANING

1. According to Lenski, what is the significance of being the answer to question 1 above?

2. If Christians are not faithful in being lights toward one another, how effective will the church be toward the culture?

3. What is the significance of the altar candles and candelabra?

4. How is a pastor a "spiritual father"?

5. Why is *akadia* so dangerous among church members?

EXPLORE IMPLICATIONS

1. So, what happens in the world if the church is not faithful in being the answer to question 1 above?

2. What is the priority St. Paul teaches in Galatians 6:9–10?

3. What is the implication that Christians are surrounded by light in church?

4. How do pastors "pay" for serving in their office?

5. How does Bonhoeffer describe how Christians need each other?

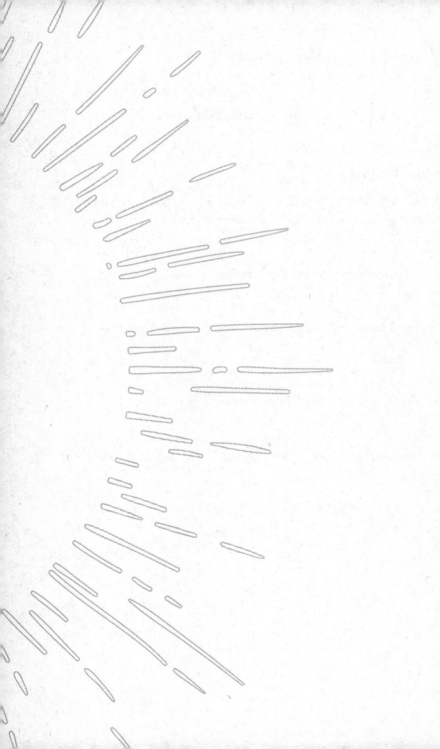

CHRIST'S LIGHT THROUGH THE CONGREGATION AND FRIENDSHIP

Children of Light Who Bring the Kingdom of God

Gerhard Uhlhorn wrote, "The whole work of our Lord may be summed up in this, that He founded upon earth the kingdom of heaven, the kingdom of God."[263] It is therefore incumbent on the followers of Christ to perpetuate this kingdom, by bringing into the world the light of Christ. Where the children of light are, there is Christ, and where the King is, there is His kingdom.

Uhlhorn describes the progression through the theme of love: "God is love, and therefore the kingdom of God is a kingdom of love: and the community of those who have been reconciled to God in Christ must hallow its whole life and conduct by love."[264] The early church understood itself as consisting of Christians being servants with their gift and in their circle (1 Peter 4:10).[265] Not every Christian serves in the office of the holy ministry; "but everyone is really and naturally a deacon, a servant of all."[266]

In the early centuries of the church—for example around the beginning of the third century—the church viewed itself as devoted to

---

263 Gerhard Uhlhorn, *Christian Charity in the Ancient Church* (New York: Charles Scribner's Sons, 1883), 57.

264 Uhlhorn, *Christian Charity*, 57.

265 Uhlhorn, *Christian Charity*, 79.

266 Uhlhorn, *Christian Charity*, 79.

good works and brought a morality to the culture that was otherwise unknown and driven by the Gospel of Christ. Light was received and light had to be reflected. It was an inevitable reflection:

> As yet institutions did not exist. There was no need of houses of hospitality, houses for foreigners, orphanages, hospitals, so long as every Christian house was an asylum for traveling brothers, and every Christian man and woman was ready to receive the indigent.[267]

History Shows the Church Can Lose Her Way

When the time of Constantine came in the early fourth century, the church became dominant and "love decayed in the multitude of nominal Christians. . . . Motives were altered."[268] Constantine bred power and influence into the church. It was as if the church "became a state within the State."[269] The church estate was losing its salt and light as it merged with the state.

By the fifth century, it was clear the church estate was losing her identity. The decay of church life was evident. Worship attendance significantly declined.[270] A new set of motives became operative. What was given to the church was no longer driven out of love for those in need but "gifts by which the individual members of the church hoped to obtain . . . intercession . . . and . . . sure to secure the favour [sic] of God."[271]

In the latter part of the Middle Ages (e.g., the time of Aquinas in the thirteenth century), the poor received extraordinary care through "an abundance of institutions of the most various kinds, what numbers of hospitals for all manner of sufferers."[272] But "Church care of the poor

---

267 Uhlhorn, *Christian Charity*, 123.
268 Uhlhorn, *Christian Charity*, 215.
269 Uhlhorn, *Christian Charity*, 225.
270 Uhlhorn, *Christian Charity*, 254.
271 Uhlhorn, *Christian Charity*, 254–55.
272 Uhlhorn, *Christian Charity*, 396–97.

entirely perished, and all charity became institutional."[273] Uhlhorn bemoaned the results:

> The transformation was complete. Men gave and ministered no longer for the sake of helping and serving the poor in Christ, but to obtain for themselves and their merit, release from purgatory, a high degree of eternal happiness . . . [and] Christian life, no longer corresponded with the gospel.[274]

With his revealing historical survey on charity in the church, Uhlhorn admonishes all Christians: "The first duty of our age is to realize in action the evangelical . . . ideas concerning charity . . . in connection with those concerning calling and work, wages and property."[275] We cannot detach faith in the Gospel received in the Divine Service from the good works that reveal the light of Christ flowing from the Gospel, which is always applied in service to the neighbor in the world. This means that our calls in the church estate do not end when we leave the sanctuary.

The Christian's Church Calling Is Full-Time

While in the prior chapter we were being mindful of the inestimable value of the Christian's service *within* the congregation, it is imperative that we not confine the Christian's church vocation to the work of the congregation itself. Both the Christian's vertical call to be a baptized child of God *as well as their horizontal call as member of the visible church in society* means that Christians are representing God, His kingdom, as well as their local congregations, all the time.

Luther said that we are all priests, "as is written in 1 Peter 2 [:9]; so that all of us should proclaim God's Word and works at every time and in every place."[276] "Laypeople are especially positioned to reach people *outside* the church," Veith explains, "by virtue of their secular

---

273   Uhlhorn, *Christian Charity*, 397.

274   Uhlhorn, *Christian Charity*, 397.

275   Uhlhorn, *Christian Charity*, 398.

276   AE 51:335.

vocations, which put them in contact with people who would never darken the door of a church."[277] Therefore the Christian's mentality must be outward into the world. Luther:

> For we are not made for fleeing human company, but for living in society and sharing good and evil. As human beings we must help one another to bear all kinds of human misfortune and the curse that has come upon us. We must be ready to live among wicked people, and there everyone must be ready to prove his holiness instead of becoming impatient and running away. . . . You have no call to pick up your feet and run away, but to stay put, to stand and battle against every kind of temptation like a knight, and with patience to see it through and to triumph.[278]

Bonhoeffer said that the Christian does not belong "in seclusion of a cloistered life but in the thick of foes."[279] It is God's will that we be scattered into the world so that "the seed of the Kingdom of God" be given to the world.[280] When those in Christ scatter the seed of the Word, then even those Christians are as seed, salt, and light to the world.

Our attitudes should be as Luther described: "The children of God do not flee from the company of evil persons; instead they seek it that they may help them. They do not want to go to heaven alone; they want to bring with them the greatest sinner, if they can."[281]

Christians Getting out There to Serve

Traci and I have been blessed to have the house we have, but it is not really our house, and it is really—at the end of the day—not even the bank's house. It is *God's* house. We just get to live in it. The same, by the way, is true about the cars we drive, the appliances we use, and all

---

277   Veith, *God at Work*, 127.
278   AE 21:86.
279   Bonhoeffer, *Life Together*, 17.
280   Bonhoeffer, *Life Together*, 18.
281   Johnson, *Day by Day We Magnify You*, 311.

the other resources the Lord has made us stewards of. Our situation is the situation of all Christians.

Apart from my call as pastor to preach the Gospel and to care for my flock with Word and Sacrament, I, along with Tracy, am also a Christian, called to be ready to serve people in need. Traci and I have been blessed with the rich experience of sharing our home and God's house on numerous occasions not just with family but also with both parishioners and non-parishioners. The length of stay has also varied from a day or two to several weeks or even months.

On one occasion as a vicar in Los Angeles, I phoned my supervisor in the middle of the night as I was trying to help a homeless person. My supervisor was a little annoyed and half-chuckled and sighed with exasperation as he tried to explain to me on the phone that while my intentions were noble, I had to learn certain boundaries. Of course, he was right. At the same time, it is amazing how the Lord can stretch such boundaries.

When Traci and I were in Texas, we were watching the news about a huge hurricane coming for the Gulf Coast. As we watched, we were both cognizant of the fact that the eye was going to strike an area in Louisiana where friends (a fellow pastor, his wife, and kids) lived. I asked Traci to call her counterpart in Louisiana. When our sister in Christ on the other end received Traci's call, Traci asked right away, "Where are you going to go?" The response was that her husband was on his knees praying when we called, asking God that very question! The pastor, however, had two elderly sisters (parishioners) in his congregation that he couldn't leave behind. Traci's response was quick, "Bring them along!"

I was blown away by how my congregation stepped up. Not only did we end up providing a part-time service position for the pastor as he stayed with us while ensuring that his family was cared for, but my congregation also provided an apartment for the elderly sisters, collected furniture for them to furnish their new digs, and ensured they had transportation for errands, midweek women's group, and worship. In addition, our congregation formed a work crew to travel out to

Louisiana to contribute to the restoration of the area. I was witnessing what Christians do beyond faithful attendance in the Divine Service.

There was also a lesson to be learned. God's people pick up on the example of their pastor—even as the pastor is inspired by his people—but both pastors and royal priests are called to live out of their comfort zones to back up Gospel proclamation with acts of mercy. Our Louisiana connection bore fruit as we reached out to others, some of whom were among thousands housed in the Astrodome in Houston. When I went there with our guest pastor, we went also with the Gospel to share.

The light of Christ, of course, isn't limited to the ministry in the states. I was fortunate to get to sit down with LCMS missionary Britt Odemba, whom the Lord is working through in Kenya, Africa. She explained to me what she is doing out there in the world:

> My main job now is working with . . . Project 24 and Christ's Care for Children Kenya sponsorship program. This is a program where we have eight boarding facilities throughout Kenya where children are able to stay at these facilities during the school year. We have sponsors in the United States who sponsor these children. The children receive a good education. The children go to a Lutheran-sponsored school, which is close to these facilities, and also attend a Lutheran church on Sundays which is also near these facilities. Each site is connected to a Lutheran church in Kenya, with either a pastor or an evangelist or a deaconess through the ELCK, the Evangelical Lutheran Church of Kenya. They are connected to these children who stay in these facilities. Currently, there are 200 children in the elementary program and stay at one of the eight facilities. And then we have 160 in high schools that stay at boarding high schools or universities. So, my job specifically is to work with the child-sponsorship program, and I am one who gathers all the information on the 360 students, takes pictures, [and] gathers information.[282]

---

282   Britt Odemba, live interview by author, Laguna Hills, CA, August 17, 2022. Anyone can sponsor a Project 24 student for $90/month, covering educational costs, books, clothing, medical care,

I also learned how Britt has been inspired through her service to the Kenyans. Many of the children served by Project 24 live in the slums of Kenya. Living there, they don't even have the assurance of food for the day. Britt explained to me that someone in our culture might think that as a result these Kenyans would be down and out, desolate, but just the opposite is often the case. Britt has met many who don't have what other people in the world think they need, and they still have joy in their lives, especially when they come to know the Lord Jesus Christ. Britt shared, "I think it's almost refreshing sometimes for Americans to realize we don't need all that, the Kenyans are still praising God . . . even though they are not sure where their next meal is going to come from. There is that trust there. It's a beautiful thing for people to come together and see that."[283]

And it is also a beautiful thing to witness Christians shining Christ's light in circumstances you just wouldn't expect. Over the years, I've valued the chance to serve law enforcement officers. During many ride-alongs, I have seen some of the stressors our police officers and sheriff deputies endure while they render a service that is easy to take for granted.

There is one officer I've known for decades, who confesses Jesus and who amazed me through some of the ways he shares the light of Christ. During a major chapter of his career, he was a leading officer in the gang division of a large city in southern California. His methodology in building bridges with gang members seemed unorthodox but was highly successful. This officer was a true peacemaker in the sense our Lord taught.

One of the things he would do when responding to certain calls and when tensions were high at the scene was enter into gang houses *without his weapon*. It was intentional and it bought him a currency of respect among the gang members that put the Christian officer in a position to help de-escalate situations that could have otherwise been deadly. It became apparent even to the gang members that he was a Christian

---

transportation, and, of course, living expenses in the boarding house. Missionary Britt Odemba can be contacted at lcms.org/odemba.

283   Odemba, interview.

man. I know he is. I have seen it in the way he worships and in the way he treats people even—if not especially—when he is in uniform.

No Need to Be Glamorous, Just Be a Friend

Being a true friend to another person is a vocation. For Christians, it is a holy calling. That is, a Christian does not have to be connected to an official ministry or organization of service to be effective in their vocation as a member of the church and kingdom of God. They can be a very bright light of love and service through the Gospel of Christ by being a friend. The call to be a friend also reminds us in the church that individual Christians are not out to change the world or system, but they focus on serving one person at a time, especially when that person is a friend.

Keller asks the question "What is friendship?" He gives the answer:

> The Bible, and particularly the book of Proverbs, spends much time describing and defining it. One of the prime qualities of a friend is constancy. Friends "love at *all* times" and especially during "adversity" (Proverbs 17:17). The counterfeit is a "fair-weather friend" who comes over when you are successful but goes away if prosperity, status, or influence wanes (Proverbs 14:20; 19:4, 6, 7). True friends stick closer than a brother (Proverbs 18:24). They are always there for you. Another of the essential characteristics of friendship is transparency and candor. Real friends encourage and affectionately affirm one another (Proverbs 27:9; cf. 1 Samuel 23:16–18), yet real friends also offer bracing critiques: "Faithful are the wounds of a friend" (Proverbs 27:5–6). Like a surgeon, friends cut you in order to heal you. Friends become wiser together through a healthy clash of viewpoints. "As iron sharpens iron, so friend sharpens friend" (Proverbs 27:17).[284]

Webb-Mitchell points out that our "friendship with one another becomes a kind of school itself—a school of charity that makes possible

---

284   Keller and Keller, *The Meaning of Marriage,* 207.

the resolution of crisis. Charity wants the best for the other, which means that there are going to be times of joy and times of challenge."[285] It might seem odd to say that charity anticipates crisis and challenge, but "Christian friends are not only to honestly confess their own sins to each other (James 5:16), but they are to lovingly point out their friend's sins if he or she is blind to them (Romans 15:14).[286] Keller says we should give our Christian friends "hunting licenses" to confront us if we are failing to live in line with our commitments (Galatians 6:1) and be willing to stir up the other, even provoking one another when necessary (Hebrews 10:24).[287]

But what about our friendships with unbelievers? Should a Christian even have close friends who do not share the faith? In this instance, we should remind ourselves that we live in all three estates at the same time, which is to say that we will always have something in common with all people, whether they are believers or not. This makes for the potential to become friends with a person without Christ. And why should this surprise us when Christ Himself would sit and eat with people known as public sinners (Mark 2:16)? The Pharisees complained since they considered such behavior as defiling, but Jesus didn't see it that way. He was making friends.

Furthermore, the estate of love that runs through the other three means that the Christian is in the position to love anyone, believer or not. The Christian friend should have overflowing compassion for their friend who is no worse a sinner than they are and yet does not yet know the love of God. Besides, many of the actions of friends described above can still be had in a relationship with an unbelieving friend. God can work through anyone to challenge our thinking for good.

Indeed, if we waited for potential friends to get past all their inadequacies before befriending them, we might go through life without any friends at all. But it is precisely here that our vocation in the church becomes especially important. We can make friends and be a friend to someone lacking what is *most important* and yet still love them.

285   Webb-Mitchell, *Christly Gestures*, 83.

286   Keller and Keller, *The Meaning of Marriage*, 115.

287   Keller and Keller, *The Meaning of Marriage*, 115.

These friends are not a project for our attempts to witness but people for whom Christ died and rose, that their lives would overflow with blessings. How about being the friend who shares this with a friend? This puts the Christian in the position to love as a friend in the very best way possible.

Christ Calls Sinners Friends

In John 15:13–15, Jesus spoke of His friendship for sinners when He said to His disciples:

> Greater love has no one than this, that someone lay down his life for his friends. You are My friends if you do what I command you. No longer do I call you servants, for the servant does not know what his master is doing; but I have called you friends, for all that I have from My Father I have made known to you.

R. C. H. Lenski explains that the original meaning "denotes an affectionate and intimate relation. . . . They remain [servants] . . . yet these . . . are treated as 'friends' by their divine Lord."[288] This new status as friends is God's gift to His disciples and reveals the Lord's desire toward sinners now in possession of His regenerating light. "Jesus never wanted his disciples to be mere [servants], blindly obeying orders, but . . . friends, intimately acquainted with all his heart's desires and all his work and mission."[289]

For these friends, the Lord will lay down His life. This seems interesting in light of Romans 5:10, which reveals that we were reconciled to Christ "while we were enemies." Middendorf points out that the "more dominant force [of our being enemies] is of God's responsive hostility toward sinful humanity, his righteous judgment or wrath (as in 1:18; 2:5)."[290] But it was precisely on the cross of Calvary that Jesus

---

288   R. C. H. Lenski, *The Interpretation of St. John's Gospel* (Minneapolis: Augsburg, 1943), 1050.

289   Lenski, *St. John's Gospel*, 1051.

290   Michael P. Middendorf, *Romans 1–8*, Concordia Commentary (St. Louis: Concordia Publishing House, 2013), 388.

absorbed this wrath in the stead of sinners and won reconciliation to God for them (Romans 5:10). This reconciliation for sinners is the basis for God's friendship for sinners.

Still, Jesus also said, "You are My friends if you do what I command you" (John 15:14). But what enables sinners to be characterized by obedience and to have love for God from which obedience springs? It is only because Jesus *is first obedient for and loving toward sinners who can do nothing to generate the life of a friend on their own.*

Jesus did not call St. Peter His friend before the three great denials of St. Peter (John 18:15–27) only to go back on His word after St. Peter denied Him. No, the Lord was still the friend of St. Peter even through the terrible darkness of his sin, and it was that friendship of the Savior that restored St. Peter three times (John 21:15–17).

Jesus enables us to be friends by grace through faith in Him alone, which means that we may also say He regards even sinners who are still enmeshed in the weakness of the flesh and imperfect obedience to be His friends. Jesus is a doctor for the sick, and He is the friend of sinners. In this way, sinners are made well and become the friends of Christ.

If Christ would befriend us like this when we were still sinful enemies, then what should ever stop a Christian from going out into the world to shine the light of Christ in genuine friendship with one who does not yet know the saving Gospel? In 1 Samuel 18:1, we get a glimpse of the great friendship between Jonathan and David: "Jonathan loved [David] as his own soul." But stop to consider that this is how deeply Christ loves the sinner. Think about how important it could be for someone without Christ to be loved by a Christian to this extent, not because of worthiness or merit, but simply as a gift. Such a gift is the light of Christ. The soul of the Savior has united itself to all humanity, and now Christians get to share this light, which is brighter than any other light in the universe.

The Medicine for Excessive Individualism

The Christian, as a friend, counters the culture of self-centeredness. The Christian friend does not love to get but to give. The world is starving for such a love and doesn't even know it. It needs to be stopped dead in its tracks by encountering Christians who insist that it is better to give than to receive (Acts 20:35).

To love this way gives witness to families that such love should be embraced and prioritized in the home. To be such a friend gives hope to citizens of the state who have grown calloused by the city seemingly fueled by greed and deceit. It is the kind of life and service—a blessed horizontal call—that can resuscitate people who have decided that such people don't exist.

The Christian friend can be a soldier in a counter-cultural movement that lives out giving our lives to serve with the Gospel, which proclaims God for sinners, and good works, which inevitably follow. Such Christians gladly make themselves a dutiful servant to all since the King of the universe has already served those same Christians in the same way and even more so.

Such Christians must also have state callings. These are a part of God's master plan to place His little Christs, His lights in the world, in every aspect of daily living. Let us now celebrate the callings Christians have in the estate that involves government and the greater culture.

CHAPTER 10 DISCUSSION GUIDE

Christ's Light through the Congregation and Friendship

UNCOVER INFORMATION

1. According to Uhlhorn, every Christian is a _____ or servant of all.

2. What happened to the church when it became dominant in the culture like a state within the state?

3. When or how often does the Christian represent the church estate?

4. What is the significance of being a Christian friend?

5. Why should Christians also be friends toward unbelievers?

DISCOVER MEANING

1. What was the significance of the Christian house in the early church?

2. Why did the church begin to decay?

3. Why is the laity especially positioned to reach people outside the church?

4. What is friendship?

5. What was the significance of friendship in the Greco-Roman world?

EXPLORE IMPLICATIONS

1. What is the Gospel of Christ supposed to produce in Christians along with faith?

2. What is the proper motivation to help those in need?

3. Why did Luther say that Christians do *not* flee the company of evil men?

4. Why is giving Christian friends "hunting licenses" a good thing?

5. What do we learn of Christ's love for us when He dies for enemies and then calls those who are still sinful His friends?

PART V

Christ's Light through State Callings

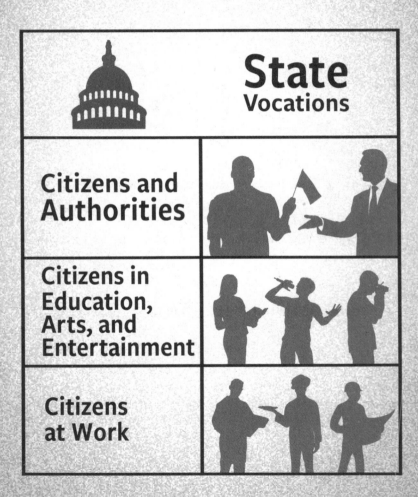

State Vocations

Citizens and **Authorities**

Citizens in Education, Arts, and Entertainment

Citizens at Work

CHRIST'S LIGHT THROUGH CITIZENS AND AUTHORITIES

Faith and the United States of America

Before we discuss the horizontal calls of Christians as citizens and authorities (at least from my perspective as a Christian who is a US citizen), we should have some clarity about the United States herself. From his visit to America in 1831, Alexis de Tocqueville made these observations:

> There is an innumerable multitude of sects in the United States. All are different regarding the worship which must be made to the Creator, but all are in agreement regarding the duties of men toward each other. Each sect thus worships God in its manner, but all sects preach the same morality in the name of God. If it is very useful to man as an individual that his religion be true, it is not the same for society. Society has nothing to fear nor to hope from the other life; and what is most important to it is not so much that all citizens profess the true religion, but that they profess some religion. In addition, all the sects in the United States are reunited in the great Christian community, and the morality of Christianity is everywhere the same.[291]

---

291   Alexis de Tocqueville, *Democracy in America*, abr. Sanford Kessler, trans. Stephen D. Grant (Indianapolis: Hackett, 2000), 132.

While we live in a state realm that maintains a certain separation between church and state, this does not mean that faith or one's personal religion does not or should not enter the political process, much less life in the culture. After the United States had only been in existence for fifty-five years, Tocqueville observed that faith and politics interact all the time, marked by *Christian* community and morality.

This is in no way, shape, or form meant to imply that Christians should seek an admixture of the church and state, or even worse, the merging of the two kingdoms of political power on the left and God's grace and church on the right. The moment this happens, the Word of God is invariably compromised as people try to unite what is unchangeable to constantly evolving political platforms. Even while God reigns over both realms, the result would create a monster, compromising and harming both sides.

On the other hand, it would also be unwise to ignore the historical correspondence between faith and the remarkable gift from God that is the American republic. To be aware of the history is to have a better sense of how our own faith as Christian authorities and citizens might remind us that what we represent is nothing strange to this nation.

Gary Scott Smith in his very helpful work on faith and the US presidency demonstrates how the separation of church and state cannot negate faith from politics in America. In 1984, President Ronald Reagan said something that even then set off, as Smith calls it, a "firestorm of protest,"[292] but he said it nevertheless, even to the delight of many other Americans who embraced his words:

> The truth is, politics and morality are inseparable. And as morality's foundation is religion, religion and politics are necessarily related. We need religion as a guide. We need it because we are imperfect, and our government needs the church because only those humble enough to admit they're

---

292   Gary Scott Smith, *Faith and the Presidency: From George Washington to George W. Bush* (New York: Oxford University Press, 2006), 4.

sinners can bring a democracy the tolerance it requires in order to survive.[293]

President Reagan was certainly not being novel. During the presidency of Dwight D. Eisenhower, national prayer breakfasts commenced, the words "under God" were added to the Pledge of Allegiance, and Congress made the phrase "In God We Trust" the national motto. Furthermore, in 1955 the president said to *Life* magazine, "Application of Christianity to everyday affairs is the only practical hope of the world."[294] And his convictions about the importance of the direct impact of faith at the national and international levels were undeniable:

> Eisenhower constantly asserted that belief in God was the surest and strongest foundation for justice and freedom. He insisted that God gave all people the same dignity and rights. Universal recognition of "the fundamental truth that all men are created equal" would set people free. Only by focusing on moral and spiritual values could the world improve race relations and increase international good will and cooperation. Without a commitment to liberty and equality, people could not achieve human brotherhood.[295]

While many Christians might find these presidential statements impressive, it would be a mistake to assume a one-for-one correspondence with Christianity per se. However, and what is important for our present consideration, no one should think that faith has not been important and complementary to the history of culture in the United States. If the United States represents anything that is good, it would be folly to discount the inestimable value of faith's impact upon her.

This is also clear in some early Supreme Court decisions. In a unanimous 1882 decision, *Church of the Holy Trinity v. United States*, the Supreme Court said, "Our laws and institutions are based upon and

---

293   Smith, *Faith and the Presidency*, 4.

294   Smith, *Faith and the Presidency*, 221–22.

295   Smith, *Faith and the Presidency*, 245.

embody the teachings of the Redeemer of mankind. . . . [I]n this sense and to this extent our civilization and our institutions are emphatically Christian. . . . [T]his is a Christian nation."[296] As late as 1925, "few challenged that notion that the United States was a Christian country . . . or argued that the state and church worked too closely together."[297]

So, what happened after 1925? Philip Hamburger states that "it is misleading to understand either eighteenth-century religious liberty or the First Amendment in terms of separation of church and state."[298] Hamburger clarifies that separation in the federal Constitution of the United States was never intended to disconnect the Christian faith from public life but rather to prevent any single sect from having undue influence over the others.[299]

But increasing separation was indeed undeniable. However, even while support for greater separation came from secularists and the non-religious, support also came from Protestant Christians who distrusted the growing influence of the Roman Catholic Church and its potential influence upon American government.[300]

Amid popular perceptions and fears, Americans were the ones who changed their understanding of religious liberty. "Increasingly, Americans conceived their freedom to require an independence from churches . . . [and to] limit such threats, Americans called for a separation of church and state, and eventually the US Supreme Court gave their new conception of religious liberty the force of law."[301]

Some have blamed President Thomas Jefferson, who was a deist, for the slide toward increased separation.[302] Jefferson strongly supported religious liberty and, while governor of Virginia, presented a bill to provide religious freedom in the state. This was opposed by Patrick

---

296   Smith, *Faith and the Presidency*, 13.

297   Smith, *Faith and the Presidency*, 13.

298   Philip Hamburger, *Separation of Church and State* (Cambridge, MA: Harvard University Press, 2002), 9.

299   Hamburger, *Separation of Church and State*, 9.

300   Hamburger, *Separation of Church and State*, 15.

301   Hamburger, *Separation of Church and State*, 17.

302   Deism is belief in a supreme being who is nevertheless detached from the world and impersonal.

Henry, who proffered an alternate bill that would have made Christianity the established religion. In response to Henry, Jefferson and Madison (eventual president James Madison) argued that the establishment of religion had a malignant and sometimes disastrous effect possibly leading to corruption and tyranny.[303] It would be, however, unfair to forget that Jefferson's original sense was designed to protect America from any single religion claiming to speak for all citizens.

Nevertheless, fast forward from 1779 to 1979, Justice Hugo L. Black epitomized the landmark Supreme Court case that year. Not only did he cite Jefferson, but he added that the "wall must be kept high and impregnable. We could not approach the slightest breach."[304] That wall he referred to is the current wall separating church and state more than ever before in the history of the United States.

Since that time, secularism has only mounted, but nothing can change the bedrock foundation of the United States, which has intrinsically included the tenets of the faith (e.g., the Ten Commandments), which have invariably reflected a moral consciousness. Whenever the church estate has helped the state, it has been when it has been true to its role as the soulish conscience of a nation. Christians who are called into state vocations still shed this light and should make the most of every opportunity to perpetuate what is good and to oppose what is harmful to and for the state.

We are not speaking of political activism that is done as a sign of misconstrued Christian sanctification but of what Christians do to be good stewards of the state, so that the state would do its job in protecting and serving the family estate and the church estate. Since the Lord has instituted all governmental authorities (Romans 13:1), which He describes as His "servant for your good" (Romans 13:4), then the Christians to whom St. Paul is writing are therefore benefiting from the government. It's true: the light of Christ is not limited to the family and the church. It is also for the state, and when the light of Christ reaches the state, it shines also through it.

---

303   Smith, *Faith and the Presidency*, 74–75.
304   Smith, *Faith and the Presidency*, 78.

The Light of Christ against Excessive Individualism

The diagnosis about America's secularism, which is demonstrated through self-aggrandizement and bent on self-love, is nothing new. It has pervaded humanity since the fall and certainly did not wait for the sexual revolution in America in the 1960s or any other cultural phenomenon for that matter.

Luther, in the Large Catechism, already mourns the state of the affairs: "The world is worse than it has ever been, and there is no government, no obedience, no loyalty, no faith, but only daring, unbridled people."[305] If you are a Christian concerned about our current culture, Luther's quote might suggest that he found a way to sneak into a time machine and look around the United States in the twenty-first century. Luther continued, as this time he spoke against coveting in the Ninth and Tenth Commandments: "Here they say, 'First come, first served,' and 'Everyone must look to his own interest; let another get what he can.'"[306] The state, however, is an extension of Law as demonstrated by its single most powerful institution: the government. And in God's Word that describes government, we don't read about much Gospel. This estate is lucidly of the Law:

> Let every person be subject to the governing authorities. For there is no authority except from God, and those that exist have been instituted by God. Therefore whoever resists the authorities resists what God has appointed, and those who resist will incur judgment. For rulers are not a terror to good conduct, but to bad. Would you have no fear of the one who is in authority? Then do what is good, and you will receive his approval, for he is God's servant for your good. But if you do wrong, be afraid, for he does not bear the sword in vain. For he is the servant of God, an avenger who carries out God's wrath on the wrongdoer. Therefore one must be in subjection,

---

305   Large Catechism I 69.
306   Large Catechism I 303–4.

not only to avoid God's wrath but also for the sake of conscience. (Romans 13:1–5)

These are not words of comfort and relief from the crushing burden of sin, but these are words of threats and the realization that God, who reigns over this estate as well, permits government to "bear the sword." To be clear, that sword was active in condemning the Lord Jesus Christ to crucifixion (John 19:16).

With this insight, Christians shine as the light of Christ *when they are exemplary examples of living rightly in this estate and in accord with the parameters God has established for it.* In this unique estate, Christians no longer live as they do toward spouse and children—and most certainly not how they live within the congregation—but even as they maintain the spiritual estate of love for all people, they must live within the structures and constrictions of the state realm.

Luther says, "Therefore [if a Christian has] an office or governmental position, [they] must be sharp and strict, [they] must get angry and punish; for here we must do what God puts into our hand and commands us to do for His sake."[307] Luther goes further to emphasize God's mask in the state: "Thus when a Christian goes to war or when he sits on a judge's bench, punishing his neighbor, or when he registers an official complaint, he is not doing this as a Christian, but as a soldier or a judge or a lawyer."[308]

But how does this shine the light of Christ? It does so by preventing the demise of the government (narrowly) and the whole state (broadly) through sin running amok. Just as the sinful flesh in a Christian must be crucified (Galatians 5:24), the sin in the world must also be resisted. And just as the cross upon the flesh is nothing but a violent act, the Christian must be strong in the state to use those resources that are in accord not with the Gospel but with the Law.

Christians must not, however, forget what they are especially defending: a state and government within the state that will not lose its bearings, so that it is responsible in serving and protecting the other

307   AE 21:23.
308   AE 21:113.

estates. And just as Christians battle their own sinful nature, they must therefore do battle against the tides in the state that would shipwreck the state in unrestrained disorder and chaos. But again, this is not done by trying to Christianize the nation or installing a theocracy. It is done by the grace of God leading Christians to live as they ought to in the state realm.

This, of course, is the significance of the review of US history above: when Christians were contributing to the state in positive ways and influential ways, the state was upholding God's Law depicting the morals that reflect beneficial order. All of this can be challenging for the Christian, however, because it means there is an acknowledgment of almost living as two different persons. And while the Christian *always* holds to the faith and *never* denies it, they *are* expressing the faith in two different and legitimate ways.

Shining in the State Is like a Paradox or Duality

Grasping the Christian faith—insofar as it can be grasped—is impossible apart from recognizing the both/and realities of Christianity. Christians

- live in what is seen and unseen.

- live with an old nature and a new nature.

- live while interacting with those who know Christ and with those who do not.

- live in the kingdom of power and the kingdom of grace.

- live in the now and the not yet (regarding the coming of Christ).

- live in the speaking of Law and the speaking of Gospel.[309]

A duality is revealed because the Christian is not only an extension of the Lord's proper work (which is love and mercy) but is also an extension of His alien work (marked by judgment and stringency). Someone might ask, "But when was Christ ever like the latter?"

---

309   Alfonso Espinosa, *Faith That Sees through the Culture.* This is the subject matter of the book.

The Passover of the Jews was at hand, and Jesus went up to Jerusalem. In the temple He found those who were selling oxen and sheep and pigeons, and the money-changers sitting there. And making a whip of cords, He drove them all out of the temple, with the sheep and oxen. And He poured out the coins of the money-changers and overturned their tables. And He told those who sold the pigeons, "Take these things away; do not make My Father's house a house of trade." His disciples remembered that it was written, "Zeal for Your house will consume Me." (John 2:13–17)

Even the Lord in this instance could not honor the money-changers as He had His parents, nor could He take them into His arms as He had the little children; and this was not the time to catechize His disciples. This time, this place, and this context were entirely different. Here, the Lord—while shining His light of holiness and truth—had to judge sin in broad daylight with zeal that must have terrified those driven out. And yet the Lord Jesus permitted *Himself* to be greatly dishonored, mistreated, and denigrated during His passion and death on the cross. This both/and can be potentially confusing.

In Luther's treatise on *Temporal Authority*, Luther was expressing this duality in respect to the Christian's relationship with civil government:

A Christian should be so disposed that he will suffer every evil and injustice without avenging himself; neither will he seek legal redress in the courts but have utterly no need of temporal authority and law for his own sake. On behalf of others, however, he may and should seek vengeance, justice, protection, and help, and do as much as he can to achieve it. Likewise, the governing authority should, on its own initiative or through the instigation of others, help and protect him too, without any complaint, application, or instigation on his own part. If it fails to do this, he should permit himself to be despoiled and slandered; he should not resist evil, as Christ's words say.[310]

---

310   AE 45:103.

But threaten the life of my unborn or recently born neighbor, then the Christian can and must defend his neighbor and serve as a citizen to influence the government to protect the innocent and helpless. Threaten the fabric of holy marriage and compromise the meaning of marriage as being between one man and one woman, then the Christian is obligated to defend the family. Permit lawlessness in the culture, then the Christian is called to fight for right policing and a responsible justice system. And if—God forbid—the church estate itself is attacked, then the Christian must say with St. Peter, "We must obey God rather than men" (Acts 5:29).

What if, however, anyone claims that the Christian is violating the separation of church and state by taking such stances? There are four things to keep in mind:

1. Separation of church and state has never stood for the separation of faith from the public square or interaction with politics.

2. No one can claim they are exempt from religious conviction impacting their worldview. Even atheists have religious convictions about God.

3. In many cases, the controversies are fundamentally moral and related to natural law and the Christian has no need to refer to theology or Scripture.[311]

4. The spiritual estate is always in play to love even enemies, seeking common ground, and being ready to give an answer for the hope that is in the Christian (the Gospel; 1 Peter 3:15).[312]

It Is Still Easy to Wish God Were More "Christian"

Things in the state realm, however, are never as black and white as we wish they were. Christians are obligated to put up with much that is

---

311   Natural law consists of moral principles governing human behavior that can be recognized independently of the Holy Bible.

312   Alfonso Espinosa, *Faith That Engages the Culture.* This is the subject matter of the book.

not good and, in many cases, dishonoring of the Lord and His Word. This is not a contradiction of Acts 5:29 but rather a real tension while upholding it.

The Scripture at Romans 13, however, is straightforward: *"Let every person be subject to the governing authorities. For there is no authority except from God, and those that exist have been instituted by God"* (Romans 13:1). And don't forget verse 6: *"for the authorities are ministers of God."* Excuse me? Do our eyes deceive us? No, they don't. The Word of God says "ministers" or servants—but not just any servants—servants representing God.

So, for example, the teachers and administrators at schools are ministers of God, politicians are ministers of God, attorneys are ministers of God, IRS and FBI agents are ministers of God, soldiers and judges are ministers of God, and even those who are our supervisors, managers, or members of boards are ministers of God. They have no authority other than the authority that God Himself has given to them in their appointed callings or at least their appointed stations if they are without faith (even then God still works through them). And that authority is holy and sacred in spite of all appearances to the contrary.

What is more, these ministers of God are **not** put into categories in Romans 13 as in category one: those ministers of God in the state realm that are also Christian and category two: those ministers of God in the state realm that are not Christian. No such distinction exists. God clumps them all together whether the civil leaders are Buddhist, satanist, agnostic, LGBTQ, atheist, Democrat, Republican, racist, capitalist, socialist, a class act with the utmost integrity, or a swindler that you can trust only as far as you can throw, no distinctions. They might all be ministers of God depending on the stations and offices God has permitted them.

This seemed untenable to those who wanted to trap the Lord as recorded in Matthew 22. They asked Jesus, "Tell us, then, what You think. Is it lawful to pay taxes to Caesar, or not?" (v. 17). The Pharisees were ready to trounce Him. If Jesus said they *should* pay taxes, then they would accuse Jesus of supporting an anti-God government. On the other side were the Herodians. They wanted Jesus to say *not* to pay taxes so that they could accuse Him of insurrection and rebellion. The Pharisees and Herodians, though vastly different, became bedfellows on this occasion so that the Lord would be trapped. They were co-belligerents brought together for the common purpose to rid themselves of Jesus Christ.

What happened next was the last thing anyone expected. Jesus asked for someone to bring out a denarius, the Roman coin for paying taxes. He then facilitated an examination of the Roman coin. It was Caesar's likeness on the coin. It was Caesar's inscription. So, Jesus declared, "Therefore render to Caesar the things that are Caesar's, and to God the things that are God's" (v. 21). Thus, we may surmise that in respect to the state realm, Jesus gave His seal of approval upon Caesar.

Hold on a second! We have all probably heard many Christians scrutinize sitting presidents of the United States in ways that they could only *begin* to scrutinize Caesar. Think of the Rome Caesar represented:

> Their one idea was Rome . . . warring and conquering. . . . The Romans from the first believed themselves called to govern the world. They looked upon all foreigners—not as barbarians, like the cultured Greeks, but—as enemies to be conquered and reduced to servitude. War and triumph were their highest conception of human glory and happiness. . . . Morality and chastity . . . yielded to vice and debauchery. Amusement came to be sought in barbarous fights of beasts and gladiators, which not rarely consumed twenty thousand human lives in a single month. . . . The huge soul of Tiberius [the Caesar at the time of Jesus] and of Nero [at the end of Paul's and Peter's ministries] was but a giant body without a soul. . . . Some of the emperors were fiendish tyrants and monsters of iniquity; and yet they were enthroned among the gods by a vote of the Senate, and altars and temples were erected for their worship.[313]

And Jesus comes along and says, "Give to Caesar what is Caesar's." He might just as well have said, "Pay your taxes and continue to support

---

313   Philip Schaff, *History of the Christian Church*, vol. 1 (Peabody, MA: Hendrickson, 1858), 80, 83.

this government." Jesus was completely and utterly unconcerned and unintimidated by the situation. He had no doubt that His heavenly Father remained in absolute control of the world order and that nothing would interfere with God's providence and will. Could it be that even Caesar was used by God for God's good purposes? There is no doubt that even Caesar was in the palm of God's hand.

God is here teaching us: "Just do what I've given you to do. Do what you're supposed to do in your vocation. The state will be the state, but *you* be faithful, and when you can right a wrong, work at it with everything you've got to serve and protect your neighbors, even when they cannot perceive the good."

We temper and contextualize this with what the Lord has permitted us as citizens in the United States in particular. We are not only called to honor our elected authorities, but we are also called to be good stewards of our citizenship as working heartily for the Lord (Colossians 3:23). US citizens are at the same time followers and leaders who can appropriate change for what honors God and truly helps the neighbor. But what if the leader of the nation himself does not know the Lord?

Such was the case regarding Cyrus, the king of Persia. This is what God said about Cyrus in Isaiah 45:4–5: "For the sake of My servant Jacob, and Israel My chosen, I call you by name, I name you, *though you do not know Me*. I am the LORD, and there is no other, besides Me there is no God; *I equip you, though you do not know Me*." Cyrus didn't know the Lord through faith. Nevertheless, he was one of God's "shepherd[s]" (Isaiah 44:28) and God's "anointed" (Isaiah 45:1). Through Cyrus, God's people would be released from exile in Babylon and, through Cyrus, the command to rebuild the temple and the Holy City would be given and executed. God worked good even through the Persian king in spite of any selfish aspirations that drove him to do what he did.

In other words, we have nothing to fear no matter who the top leader or leaders may be. We might think God could be more "Christian" by permitting "more Christian" leaders, laws, and policies, but the Lord sees more than we do. Our call is to be faithful in our horizontal calls as we abide in our baptismal grace in Christ.

Faith and Love in the Third Estate

When so much of what we see in the realm of the state and general culture seems against the objective faith once delivered, then we require subjective faith in our hearts, holding to Christ, to continue to walk by faith and not by sight (2 Corinthians 5:7). Luther keeps it simple for us regarding the Fourth Commandment: "So just do what is your duty. Let God manage how He will support you and provide enough for you. Since He has promised it and has never lied yet, He will not be found lying to you [Titus 1:2]."[314] To live this way requires faith, which will always be given through the Word and Sacraments, even to live faithfully in the state realm.

Miroslav Volf and Ryan McAnnally-Linz, however, also remind us that our vocations in the state can be considered as exciting and as making a difference:

> Now each citizen is a member of the sovereign people bound together to a constitution. As a consequence, Christian obedience to political authorities is not merely regulated by a more fundamental obedience to God but is also compatible with efforts to alter political society's course. Political change is no longer simply a top-down affair but a responsibility of all adult members of the community.[315]

Volf and McAnnally-Linz lay out five imperatives that should shape the Christian's engagement with the culture in the third estate: (1) Seek peace in the sense of well-being for the community. (2) Defend the poor. (3) Don't act out of fear, and resist fear-based arguments that breed mistrust, hostility, and violence. (4) Seek the truth and tell it, that is, we do not ignore racism, ethnic or religious prejudice, and injustice. (5) Love your neighbors. And, of course, here we are led back

---

314   Large Catechism I 165.

315   Miroslav Volf and Ryan McAnnally-Linz, *Public Faith in Action: How to Engage with Commitment, Conviction, and Courage* (Grand Rapids, MI: Brazos Press, 2016), 22.

to the spiritual estate of the love that drives us to serve our neighbors in all of the estates.[316]

Two more points: first, Volf and McAnnally-Linz also help us consider how faith and love check our service in the state as we interact with our neighbors. It is helpful to be aware of two kinds of respect: one of them is *appraisal respect* and the other is *recognition respect*. "Appraisal respect is positive evaluation of somebody's achievements or virtues. . . . In contrast, recognition respect is elicited by the worth someone has simply by being what she is."[317]

The distinction is helpful as Christians live out their state callings. We might not be able to establish appraisal respect for another person's position or lifestyle, but we can still maintain recognition respect while reminding ourselves that for this one, too, the Lord died and rose and is dearly loved by God.

And finally, we are reminded by Volf and McAnnally-Linz that both "theologians and philosophers have identified three aspects of virtuous compassion: feeling, thinking, and doing."[318] As those who share the light of Christ, our compassion—even toward our most ardent opponent in the state realm—should strive not only to feel the pain of the other, and to think about what may be causing it, but also, and most importantly, to actively care for the person in any way we can. In our culture today, to disagree means lines of demarcation, hostility, and avoidance. But Jesus did not run away from people but rather sought them out. Light must find the neighbor.

---

316   Volf and McAnnally-Linz, *Public Faith in Action*, 134–35. This is my paraphrase.

317   Volf and McAnnally-Linz, *Public Faith in Action*, 200.

318   Volf and McAnnally-Linz, *Public Faith in Action*, 209.

CHAPTER 11 DISCUSSION GUIDE

Christ's Light through Citizens and Authorities

UNCOVER INFORMATION

1. How did Alexis de Tocqueville characterize America?

2. What did the 1882 Supreme Court decision of *Church of the Holy Trinity v. United States* say?

3. What is the government supposed to do for Christian congregations?

4. Just as Christians must battle their sinful nature, what else must they battle within the state?

5. What is the Christian to do against lawlessness in the state?

DISCOVER MEANING

1. While we should neither merge nor confuse church and state, why is it also wrong to ignore the correspondence between faith and America?

2. What was the original sense and meaning of the separation between church and state?

3. Is Romans 13:1–5 Law or Gospel? Explain your answer please.

4. In what way are Christians living in a duality while belonging to both church and state?

5. Why is the Christian still called to honor authorities that are not themselves Christian?

EXPLORE IMPLICATIONS

1. How does the quote of President Ronald Reagan speak to the church being as a conscience to the state?

2. How is the church true to the state?

3. When are Christians "exemplary examples of living rightly" within the state?

4. What does Jesus clearing out the temple teach us about the importance of being salt and light in the state?

5. Why should the Christian never fear whoever is in authority?

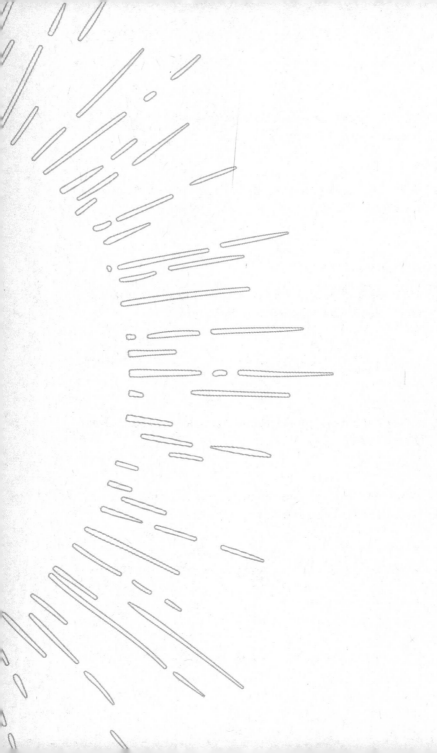

CHRIST'S LIGHT THROUGH CITIZENS IN THE GREATER CULTURE

Invaluable Servants Who Educate and Form Us

Where would we be without our good teachers? My earliest years of school were a time for recreation and socialization, but something was added to these in third grade. He was a gentleman and sophisticated, and he was my teacher. He fascinated me, and when he invited me to join the chess club, I was all in. A rough and tumble kid was given the occasion to learn to focus and concentrate. Because of my third grade teacher, I started turning a corner I didn't know existed.

There were only three teachers between kindergarten and eighth grade who made indelible impressions upon me. The second one was the very next year in fourth grade. I don't know what it was in her voice. We were lining up outside the classroom, and I was horsing around. What she said to me was more than the words *but the way she said it*: "Grow up, Alfonso!" Her words came with a look. The look said, "I expect better from you!"

Then came the day that she got all over me for missing a spelling word. I couldn't grasp what she was doing in keeping me after class. She was drilling into me that I could be more than I was. She handed me some white chalk and said, "Spell out the word one hundred times." I've never forgotten how to spell *important* since.

Fast forward to eighth grade. She was no-nonsense and strict, and she brought out the best in me. To this day, I don't know what she saw in me, but I expressed my gratitude decades later by writing to her (and she wrote back). Somehow, she just knew what I could do. Her confidence in me made me expect more of myself. By the end of the year, she led me to be class valedictorian.

High school was a blur. There were good teachers there too, but my friends and social life commanded my energy, as well as, quite frankly, football, basketball, track as a weight man in shot put and discus, and student government. I coasted to graduate in the top ten of my class, but my bad academic habits meant I got off to a terrible start in college. Humbled by this, I went to a new school for a new beginning: Concordia University in Irvine (at the time, Christ College Irvine).

I finally started to value higher education, and three men there commenced forming me in ways unexpected. One inspired passion and energy; the other inspired reading and scholarship; and the third, meticulous research and precision. All of them were doctors, and I started to pattern myself as a conglomerate of the three.

Graduate-level studies at seminary honed me. There were three new professors I have emulated to this day (coming up on thirty-two years since seminary graduation). The first one was a pastor-theologian, a man of peace and gentleness with a rapier mind; the second also a scholar, but anything but stuffy and unafraid to say what needed to be said; and the third, a man of joy and peace who knew his Hebrew and took God's Word and applied it in the most personal ways. He taught with laughter and at other times with resolute conviction and authority.

Since I entered the parish, my parishioners have been my teachers, and through a second graduate program, I had another set of good Christian professors equipping me, this time in Christian apologetics with a standout professor showing me the complementary nature of God's Word and science. Then came my doctoral supervisor in England. He might be the one that has taught me more than anyone to never underestimate the providence of the Lord. Theologically, we might have been as far apart as one could imagine, but we had good chemistry, and he took me to the next level of research and writing. He was an incredible blessing to me.

Christ's Light That Draws Out Light

Luther wrote in the Large Catechism, "Therefore, this is a true and good saying of old and wise people: 'To God, to parents, and to teachers we can never offer enough thanks and compensation.'"[319] Volf and McAnnally-Linz celebrate the import of *education*:

> Education, as John Henry Newman (1801–90) put it, is "a higher word." The etymology of the Latin word *educatio* suggests rearing or bringing up a child. It isn't so much about acquiring knowledge and skill to succeed in this or that endeavor as it is about cultivating wisdom so as to "succeed" as a human being.[320]

We are reminded that the "old phrase for [education] was the 'cultivation of the soul.' Done well, character formation requires attachment between student and teacher and a teacher attuned to the particularities of each student."[321] What a fantastic inroad and opportunity to serve others with the light of Christ. The best teachers never just "teach" the subject matter, they enter the lives of their students and cultivate learning by cultivating a relationship; treating the students as God would have us treat them: as His gifted people ready to be drawn out.

The Connection to the Other Estates

Volf and McAnnally-Linz also point out that communities other than schools are also vitally important for education. They are specific in mentioning the most prominent "others": families and churches.[322]

Webb-Mitchell also sees the inestimable value of a holistic view of where education happens, and it is emphasized in *communities*. He mentions that Immanuel Kant "provided the intellectual foundation for the shift to radical individualism," that is, the autonomous person has access through observation, experimentation, and careful reflection

319   Large Catechism I 130.
320   Volf and McAnnally-Linz, *Public Faith in Action*, 51.
321   Volf and McAnnally-Linz, *Public Faith in Action*, 51.
322   Volf and McAnnally-Linz, *Public Faith in Action*, 55.

to discover the truth in the world.[323] But Webb-Mitchell argues that the problem "may not be individualism per se but self-centeredness," and then he goes on to say that the church is responsible for teaching people "a sense of 'we-ness' in the life of the church, family, and any other social setting."[324]

And here we are reminded of the inextricable nature of the three estates according to the plan of God. Luther expressed this common sense for the light of God working through the state:

> It therefore behooves the [city] council and the authorities to devote the greatest care and attention to the young. Since the property, honor, and life of the whole city have been committed to their faithful keeping, they would be remiss in their duty before God and man if they did not seek its welfare and improvement day and night with all the means at their command. Now the welfare of a city does not consist solely in accumulating vast treasures, building mighty walls and magnificent buildings, and producing a goodly supply of guns and armor. . . . A city's best and greatest welfare, safety, and strength consist rather in it having many able, learned, wise, honorable, and well-educated citizens.[325]

Luther did not mince words on the magnitude of this responsibility to educate: "It is highly necessary, therefore, that we take some positive action in this matter before it is too late; not only on account of the young people, but also in order to preserve both our spiritual and temporal estates."[326]

Education That Is the Light of Truth

The Christian faith holds to objective truth. Any assertion that comes out of our mouths, if it is true, is only true because it corresponds to

---

323   Webb-Mitchell, *Christly Gestures*, 13.
324   Webb-Mitchell, *Christly Gestures*, 14.
325   AE 45:355–56.
326   AE 45:371.

a real situation or is logically coherent, such as the results in mathematics. The point here is that what cannot be relied upon as truth is when I say that something is true *simply because I say so, or because it is true "for me."*

C. S. Lewis argues that good education will not stray from the standard that what is inculcated to students is consistent with the objective, what might also be referred to as "Natural Law or Traditional Morality or the First Principles of Practical Reason . . . [and that this] is not among a series of possible systems of value."[327] Lewis says that if this single thing is rejected, since it "is the sole source of all value judgements," then, "all value is rejected."[328]

If such objective knowing is eliminated in education, then "education" becomes a perpetuation of superstition. Lewis bemoans the consequences: "If my duty to my parents is a superstition, then so is my duty to posterity. If justice is a superstition, then so is my duty to my country or my race. If the pursuit of scientific knowledge is a real value, then so is conjugal fidelity."[329]

Lewis also refers to this universal objective truth as "the doctrine of objective value . . . [through which] certain attitudes are really true, and others really false, to the kind of thing the universe is and the kind of things we are."[330] It is therefore incumbent in our schools that we do not give in to relativism. If we do, Lewis warns that we will "remove the organ and demand the function. We make men without chests and expect of them virtue and enterprise. We laugh at honour [sic] and are shocked to find traitors in our midst."[331]

Lewis's final warning in *The Abolition of Man* is if people continue to put their own mastery and power ahead of everything else, untethering themselves from universal truth and morals; and if people become their

---

327 C. S. Lewis, *The Abolition of Man: How Education Develops Man's Sense of Morality* (New York: MacMillan, 1947), 56.

328 Lewis, *The Abolition of Man*, 56.

329 Lewis, *The Abolition of Man*, 56.

330 Lewis, *The Abolition of Man*, 29.

331 Lewis, *The Abolition of Man*, 35.

own authority without any other authority, then the final conquest of man will be the abolishing of mankind itself.[332]

The inroad here for connecting education as a light from and to Christ is that God is not in the realm of superstition but is the one who is the truth (John 14:6). God is known via the observation of creation (Romans 1) and the experience of conscience (Romans 2). Moreover, Christ's person and work is substantiated by recorded history and primary witnesses, not the stuff of fairy tales and myth. When instructors and students are faithful in the pursuit of truth in the state realm, they are in the position to find that the same Creator and Preserver who supplies truth in the state is the one who does the same for the family and the church.

Being a Student Is a Calling

I considered myself fortunate to meet with Scott Ashmon, the senior vice president and provost of Concordia University Irvine.[333] His sublime understanding of holy vocation came out almost immediately when he described his approach for living out his baptismal life through "what Christ has done in me, for me, done to me, that then moves me in this particular calling [his various horizontal calls]."[334]

It was also refreshing how succinctly he could describe the expansive nature of his call at the university: "I can love and care for my neighbors, and those neighbors are those right next door to me, the colleagues who are faculty, the colleagues who are staff, the neighbors who are students, the neighbors who are the parents of the students, the relatives, and those they're going to be impacted by."[335]

Regarding that very last part of what he said: it was the first time in my research that I had encountered the idea that our neighbors include those who will be impacted by those we serve—people we may never meet.

---

332   Lewis, *The Abolition of Man*, 63–77.
333   Scott Ashmon, live interview by author, Zoom video call, September 12, 2022.
334   Ashmon, interview.
335   Ashmon, interview.

I was, however, especially impressed by how Ashmon views his service to the students at the university. The students are taught about their vocation through the teaching of their different *P*s:

> Love your *parents* by taking studying seriously, engaging, because they've invested so much in you. . . . The *public* supports you in this . . . honor the public in this because of their care and support and expectations of you. Your *peers* . . . to be a student, support other students. How can you be of assistance to your peers? Think of the people you also serve in the *past*, to the degree that we inherit treasures and traditions and riches from the past. How do we honor that and learn from that, if we read history; how do we love that person who's in the past? Read about them, have an open mind to them, be charitable to their views, put the best construction on their actions. [This] prepares you to love the neighbor today too. There's the *progeny*: what you do today sets you up for what you do tomorrow. Then there's loving *your own person*. Enrich yourself emotionally, intellectually, physically. [This] is a form of the care of the self. And [this] can bring you great joy, to be able to discover God's world and be in your place in it and strengthen [others].[336]

Again, Ashmon expanded the view of the neighbors we serve in vocation. There are neighbors we have never met but whose writings or inventions have touched our lives. They touch us through the corridor of time and contribute to our formation going into the future. When we avail ourselves of their influence, we honor them and become better equipped to serve the neighbors yet to be encountered. The opportunities to love our neighbors are endless.

Ashmon also described the distinctiveness of a *Christian* university to be what he described as a "demystifier, in a way," elaborating, "As our culture goes more and more post-Christian, people are less and less informed about what Christianity is in the church and the tradition

---

336   Ashmon, interview.

in the church is to be truth tellers in a winsome way. There is a saying here at the university, 'If people don't know something, they're likely to fill it with a wrong answer.' So, we want to tell truthful rumors."[337]

Callings That Entertain and Inspire

Remember the officer assigned to the gang unit? He once told me that one of his weekly rituals was to go to the cinema to watch a movie. It was a significant way for him to try to unwind and decompress when he had a day off.

I could relate to him. Traci and I do the same thing. Admittedly, we struggle to find a good movie, but when we do, it is a gift to be able to laugh or tear up or feel pumped up by what we see and hear on the big screen.

But have you ever noticed the credits that come after movies nowadays? I am awestruck by the immensity of some film projects. I am still not completely clear as to what "key grips" are all about, but they are part of the army required to produce a movie. We are witnessing the result of a ton of work by a ton of people. Every one of them—when they combine what they do with faith and love—is serving in a holy calling.

This is the case with a former parishioner and someone I got to see again for a recent interview, Lynn-Holly (Johnson) Givens. Lynn-Holly has been cast in several Hollywood productions, including one of the James Bond films.[338] Before her acting vocation, she was a US National Figure Skating silver medalist and national freestyle champion. Her film debut was the original *Ice Castles,* in which she played a figure skater in the romantic drama.

When Lynn-Holly moved out to California to start her film career (from age 19 to about 30), she described her experience as "exhilarating" but quickly learned that in the "movie business . . . money talks. . . . When I was working a lot and it was my birthday, my apartment was filled with flowers sent from producers and studios left and right. . . . And then next year my birthday comes. I got nothing. Oh, I get it

---

337   Ashmon, interview.

338   Lynn-Holly (Johnson) Givens, live interview by author, July 7, 2022. The James Bond movie was *For Your Eyes Only.*

now. Wow. Yeah, I got it now. Now I understand what the business is all about."[339]

But she also discovered that *that* is not the *only* thing the business is about. After her screen test for *Ice Castles*, she was given the whole script, and the director really wanted her. Going over the script, she saw a topless scene. From a pay phone, she called the director saying, "I will do it if you take out the scene." The director was thrilled and gave every indication that he would fight to get the scene taken out. It was after filming started, however, that the rest of the drama started. Lynn-Holly recounted:

> We were probably a third of the way into [the movie] . . . and I show up for work one day and the director says, "So, we kind of rewrote this scene, so here's the new scene and you're going to be over here, and this is where he's going to take your top off." And I said, "What?!" . . . I just giggled and said, "I am not doing that! No way! I'm not doing that!" . . . So, he stormed out and [then] the *producer* came up to me and balled me out and [once again] I said, "I'm not doing that!" And he yelled and screamed, shut down production for the day. . . . The next day he came to my hotel room and asked, "Are you doing it?" I said, "No, I am not." *Another* day of not shooting. The next day he came back to say, "You're costing me 25,000 bucks every day . . . but I kept saying, "No, I'm not doing it."[340]

And she never did, but she *did* finish a movie that was loved by audiences, and it has delighted Lynn-Holly that the movie was a hit for whole families to enjoy together. It is also a movie that today Lynn-Holly is proud of, knowing she kept her God-given convictions. Not only did she stand by her faith, but she gave notice to the whole production team—and during her Hollywood days, to the whole industry—that not *everyone* in Hollywood was going to go along with the crowd. What was more, she would never have to be ashamed of the movies she

339 Givens, interview.
340 Givens, interview.

made and who would see them years later. It was most certainly one way that she loved those she served as an actress, living with honorable standards and values.

Previously we've considered how from the outside looking in what Christians do in their horizontal calls is hardly distinguishable from what non-Christians do, but when you back up and look at the whole picture, there is a light that Christians bring into the culture that would otherwise never be detected.

Never Underestimate Christ's Light in the Culture

When it comes to the arts, the Lord has provided, and continues to provide, tremendous inroads for the horizontal calls of God's people to shine the light of Christ. Some of them are far-reaching and have immense impact on the culture.

Johann Sebastian Bach's influence on music is, of course, immeasurable. He was a musician dedicated to the glory of Christ, but even secularists who might know nothing of his faith will recognize his music. To this day, one can find that modern musicians from a variety of genres borrow from the inexhaustible expressions of his love for God.

Musicals in such cities as New York, Los Angeles, Chicago, or London can be superb examples of the finest art forms, and among the most popular musicals is *Les Misérables*. Victor Hugo's classic is a powerful testimony of grace leading to transformation and the sacrifice of love that follows.

In 1981, the movie *Chariots of Fire* won the Oscar for Best Picture. It includes the true story of Eric Liddell, missionary to China, who was also a Scottish sprinter competing in the 1924 Summer Olympics in Paris. He refused to run in the heats of his strongest race, the 100 meters, because they were held on a Sunday. He ran instead during the week in the 400 meters and won gold.

As a cultural observer, I believe our sports world says a lot about the state of our culture. On one occasion, though, I wondered how a sports icon might influence people through what otherwise seemed to be sincere and real repentance. Of course, only the Lord knows the heart, but having said that, I was impressed with what I saw.

Kobe Bryant had become one of my all-time favorite athletes. His ferocity and work ethic put him in a class by himself. Whatever he may have lacked in size, he made up for by sheer will and uncanny ability. But what made me a bigger fan was how he responded to the firestorm he went through after allegations occurring in 2003 that also led him to confessing his infidelity toward his wife, Vanessa. He confessed his sin in front of everyone and rededicated himself to do the right thing. His new chapter in life was marked by new tattoos, and one of them was Psalm XXVII (Kobe used the Roman numerals) placed on his right arm. This is verse one:

> The LORD is my light and my salvation; whom shall I fear? The LORD is the stronghold of my life; of whom shall I be afraid? (Psalm 27:1)

Kobe and his eldest daughter, Gianna, were among seven others who died in a helicopter crash on January 26, 2020. That Sunday was the Third Sunday after the Epiphany. Guess what the assigned lectionary Psalm was for that Sunday in many churches. Psalm 27.

Kobe's so-called "Mamba Mentality"—his drive and self-discipline to be the very best—is a thing for the secular realm, or is it simply that? Isn't it also true that if we are going to do anything, that we should do it as if serving the Lord as we love Him with all our might?

King David testified to this when he danced around the ark with all his might (2 Samuel 6:14). And the good stewardship of our horizontal calls means that we ought to strive to multiply God's talents put into our care (Matthew 25:14–30), not for ourselves but for our neighbors. Christ is worthy of receiving all our might.

You Don't Have to Be a Celebrity

The lights of Christ come from every direction. "Pastor's Syndrome" is a real thing. Because pastors are so sedentary—sitting while visiting, giving pastoral counsel, hearing confession, writing sermons, and doing what I'm doing right now in writing this book—pastors easily gain too much weight. Not a good prescription for trying to stay in shape.

Since 2013, however, I've had a tae kwon do instructor who has been nothing but a blessing to me. If exercising was left to my own motivation and self-discipline, I would be in big trouble, but he has helped me tremendously—helping me in a way that has benefited everything else I do. He is a Christian. We have even prayed together. Christ might even be shining through him when we are sparring.

Winding back the clock to my year-long vicarage when I was only 24, I went into an urgent care because I had bronchitis, not exactly the best thing for preaching and teaching. I will never forget God in that mask wearing a white coat. He treated me and surely noticed my clerical collar. I could not have known what was about to happen. The doctor completely switched gears, making it known that he was a brother in Christ. And then he admonished me: I had to take care of myself if I would effectively serve God's people. He held my hand and prayed over me.

Traci and I got referred to a contractor who has helped us with our house over the years on numerous occasions. His work is top-shelf, and he made it known from the beginning that because of my calling as a pastor, he would extend a discount. He has always been there for us.

At the shop where I take my car is a brother in Christ who basically pulls out the red carpet whenever I have a problem. Taking cars in for repair is painful, but when I must take my car in, I always look forward to seeing my friend who I trust and rely upon. He is someone I have prayed with.

The printer in our town is someone I've been working with now for a dozen years. We don't have our own church printer, so we've been his regular customers, delivering all our services to him. He keeps our bulletin covers in stock and then produces the final version. He is the most reliable businessman I know, and, on many occasions, he has run our funeral bulletins at no cost. The frosting on top of the cake? He delivers the finished bulletins to my residence every single week.

Christians live out their horizontal vocations and they look just like non-Christians who work just as hard in similar stations. The light of Christ through the Christian for the neighbor is for the most part invisible, but not completely. There is one distinctive element:

what the Christian does is never just about work but always about the people they serve.

The Light of Christ in Our Work

Since the sinful flesh continually tempts us to complain about work, it is easy to forget that when the Lord finished His work, He deemed that the result "was very good" (Genesis 1:31). In that instance, work was sanctified with inestimable worth. We may now catch God's vision for work: that its result in life for us, our neighbor, and the world would be very good.

It must be important because, by God's ordaining, the ratio given for our work and rest is 6:1. Rest is important indeed, and most certainly undervalued in our culture today, but it is God who has ascribed our work as a priority. It must be that He desires we use our God-given gifts, skills, and abilities for good. When we work this way, it is as if we present an offering to God, one which He does not need but our neighbor does.[341]

We must keep in mind, however, that here we are not treating "work" as synonymous with "job." Our jobs are one vocation among many, but our service in all estates are part and parcel of our work.

Even when it comes to the church estate, while Christians know the sweetest rest in receiving the Word and Sacraments of Christ for forgiveness and eternal life, I know many leaders in the church estate who put in long hours of volunteer work for the congregation. The work in the church estate represents a significant cross for any Christian who is committed to the well-being of the congregation.

It was also a wise person who admitted that a good marriage takes hard work, even in the face of all the joys it should bring—and no one will doubt that running a household is work. My wife, Traci, is one of the hardest workers I know. She doesn't get a paycheck, but she keeps our house running, and without her, I couldn't do what I do.

Nevertheless, work—all our work, including the work we do at our jobs—is still a form of worship and Luther saw this:

341 Wingren, *Luther on Vocation*, 10.

> All godly people have some definite times at which they
> pray, meditate on holy things, and teach and instruct their
> people in religion; nevertheless, even when they are not doing
> these things and are attending either to their own affairs or
> to those of the community in accordance with their calling,
> they remain in good standing and have this glory before God,
> that even their seemingly secular works are a worship of God
> and an obedience well pleasing to God.[342]

We learn from St. Paul that Christians conduct a "spiritual worship"
(Romans 12:1). This occurs whenever the Christian does anything in
faith, even when that which is done feels mundane or appears irrelevant
to the kingdom of God. Much to the contrary, when what we do is in
accord with our God-given vocations within the God-given estates—in
faith—then the work is always relevant and always worship.

Our problem, however, is that we have many doubts about our
work, our jobs included. We often feel as though they are neither good,
relevant, significant, nor enjoyable, so how can we view them as worship
to God and a blessing to our neighbor? While we are not here denying
the instances when changes must be made, the sinful tendency is to
run away for the wrong reasons.

We often shoot ourselves in the foot for the unrealistic expecta-
tions we have about our work. We quickly forsake the Lord's vision
and purpose for our work when we assume that work exists for our
self-gratification and most assuredly what we expect it should be. If
we do not perceive our work as worthy of our goals and abilities, then
frustration reigns.

Consider, however, the public ministry of our Savior, Jesus. Was
His work ever resisted, frustrated, rejected, dismissed, falsely labeled,
or misconstrued? Clearly it was. And yet, He was doing exactly what
He was supposed to be doing and what was undoubtedly radiant and
beautiful in the sight of God. Of course, we will also experience frustration. And sometimes it is the frustrating part that turns out to be

---

342   AE 2:349.

the greatest blessing about our work. When we continue to serve by loving our neighbors right through the frustrations, then the cross is killing our self-centered selves and our ludicrous individualism. Here is Bonhoeffer on this point:

> Work plunges men into the world of things. The Christian steps out of the world of brotherly encounter into the world of impersonal things, the "it"; and this new encounter frees him for objectivity; for the "it"-world is only an instrument in the hand of God for the purification of Christians from all self-centeredness and self-seeking. The work of the world can only be done where a person forgets himself, where he loses himself in a cause, in reality, the task, the "it." In work the Christian learns to allow himself to be limited by the task, and thus for him the work becomes a remedy against the indolence and sloth of the flesh. . . . But this can happen only where the Christian breaks the "it" to the "Thou," which is God, who bids him work and makes that work a means of liberation from himself.[343]

That is, God uses work like the hammer of the Law to crush our self-centeredness in life. It makes us focus on the need at hand and puts our radical individualism aside so that we might help and serve our neighbor. But Bonhoeffer maintains that we need to recognize what is going on: the work is not just a bleak reality, drudgery that is without meaning. No, it is rather what God has given us to do, so that the work takes on a dignity it never had before.

If we are frustrated, we may be frustrated, but without sinning. Instead, by the grace of God, we can bear that cross of frustration and still make a difference in the lives of the people we are serving. This is good as we more reflect the image of Jesus. This is sanctification: we find it in our callings in all three estates, and it is here where we learn that love runs through them all.

---

343   Bonhoeffer, *Life Together,* 70.

Real Life Lights of Christ

I was excited to get some insight from Tom Garrett, an attorney, who walks the walk of his confession of Jesus. The Lord has blessed his practice and there is no doubt that he understands the significance of Christian vocation. I asked him about how his Christian faith impacts what he does in holy vocation as an attorney, and this is what he said:

> It transcends my daily living and vocation, and, as a result, controls how I go about doing the Lord's work. People who come to me for legal counsel are each unique not only in terms of their legal issues but also in their respective personalities, their mental approach to their problems, which then impacts their real or imagined expectations of me and my job. Sometimes people are harsh and difficult. I understand this because I realize human frailties, and I do not judge them. We focus on the issues of the case, and I can minimize the emotions and work towards the resolution of the problem which brought them to me in the first place. My conscious approach is that it is not about me [but] about helping my neighbor as the Lord would have me do.[344]

Here I heard firsthand testimony from a Christian man who has learned not to make it about himself but to focus on the need of his neighbor before him. When clients come in and they are harsh or difficult, it can't be pleasant, but he will not permit such dispositions to divert him from serving his neighbor to the glory of God.

Todd Martin is another professional who shines the light of Christ. He is a practicing obstetrician gynecologist in Lincoln, Nebraska. When we spoke, he reinforced God's Word about the fully human little person in the womb: "You know, that pregnant person I have, I technically have *two* patients, mom *and* baby in the womb . . . [and] the number one priority is to hand you a beautiful, healthy baby and if we have

---

344   Tom Garrett, live interview by author, telephone call, August 22, 2022.

to divert from the path we set on in order to accomplish goal number one, that's what we'll do."[345]

Moreover, he also expressed a sublime understanding of vocation: "There was a plaque above one of the scrub sinks . . . [where] I was training . . . [that had a prayer on it] called *the surgeon's prayer*: knowing that God is working through your hands, you are an instrument for Him. And that was always a really nice reminder that even when procedures take a wild turn, you know that you're not working alone."[346] And when things *do* take a wild turn, then the cross is real. Todd shared about one of those times:

> A young couple, first pregnancy, [and] unfortunately at their 20-week scan things were obviously very, very wrong. They . . . delivered [their son] at about 35 weeks. Their little boy . . . had trisomy 18 [Edwards' syndrome], which is incompatible with life, [and] unfortunately he did not survive the labor process and was born at peace. And throughout this process, you know 20 weeks to 35 weeks, we have 15 weeks to where [the mother, father,] and I talked about [their son] and about what might be seen or might be experienced during the process of labor and delivery. They are very well founded in their faith, and leading up to the delivery, I had a lot of apprehension, I had a lot of this tension, kind of wondering what it was going to be like . . . [but] the delivery in the moment, the time with [the parents and baby] after delivery . . . it was amazing grace.[347]

Here was a Christian doctor traveling through the storm with these young parents and shining the light of Christ's love, compassion, and tenderness. These are moments when the work presents a cross, but then this testimony: "it was amazing grace." That's the light of Christ.

I was also blessed to speak to Steve Furbacher, a corporate executive who has worked for more than one company. Throughout his successful

---

345   Todd Martin, live interview by author, Zoom video call, August 5, 2022.

346   Martin, interview.

347   Martin, interview.

career, he was also determined to live his faith. He told me what his Christian father had taught him, something that helped him to not be afraid of doing the right thing as a Christian man:

> He said you know you're going to find yourself in situations and when you know it's not right . . . he said just remember: you know how to find a job if you lose the one you have because you found the one you have. And you can always put food on the table. He used McDonald's as an example. He said because you can go to McDonald's and flip hamburgers and put food on the table . . . do what's right.[348]

What Steve learned from his father was not just a theory. One of the companies he worked for was headed for bankruptcy and Steve was the only executive left, even after 90 percent of the board got replaced. Steve was untouched, though, because a separate unit of the organization he ran was delivering results. He would not compromise while "fully recognizing that my boss along the way could at any time say you're not playing the game, you're out."[349]

Then a new CEO came and made more changes. The US attorney's office got involved and was going after the bad actors in the company from the prior debacle. And this is where we pick up with Steve's own telling:

> There was a woman who, at the time, was now working for me because the project on which she was working got moved into the organization for which I was responsible. At that time previously when all the mess happened, she was in the part of the organization that had all the problems. . . . She was a minion on a team of people who did the deal that created the biggest problem for [the company]. . . . She didn't drive it; she was on the team. The US attorney wanted to talk to her. . . . He threatened [my boss] and then [my boss] threatened me. . . . He

---

348   Steve Furbacher, live interview by author, Zoom video call, August 2, 2022.

349   Furbacher, interview.

said, "You need to deliver her and if she doesn't, she's gone."
I said, "No, we're not going to do that." I said, "Let me handle
it." He said, "No, she's going to do it." I said, "You're going to
have to go over and through me to get to her. Because what
you want to do is wrong. You have threatened her, and she's
scared, and now you want me to threaten her again." I went
back to his office. I said, "I'm not doing it. Do what you want
with me and her, but I'm standing in the way." I went home
not knowing if I had a job or not. . . . [The next] morning, [my
boss] called me in and had the HR manager there . . . suffice it
to say, we left. The HR manager walked out with me, and she
said, "I've never seen you like that. I'm glad there was a table
between you and [the boss], I think you would have attacked
him." . . . [My boss called me while I was driving home and in
his own way apologized]. He asked me, "Will you see if you
can make this happen?" I said, "Sure. On my terms." He said,
"Fine." I went and talked to the woman, and I assured her that
I had her back and went through the criteria. I said, "Here's
the conditions under which I think you ought to be willing
to do it. I'd be more than happy to advocate those to you with
[the CEO] and with the US attorney. We went through all that
and it came out just fine.[350]

This is a real life example of what we have been discussing. Steve
bore a cross through this crisis. He defended his neighbor (the woman
under fire), and he also loved his CEO neighbor by showing him the
right way, even if it meant going head-to-head with him. He put himself
out there and could have lost his job, but Steve knew what was more
important.

Christians shine light in the state realm by doing what is right. When
they do, they testify to the consciences given to them and all people by
the living God. Even when people around us are sinfully stubborn and
driven by a thirst for power, we can stand against them—in love—and

say, "No, this is wrong." When we remain steadfast in this way, we should not be surprised that the Lord might forge a hearing also for the Gospel to be shared.

Attorney, doctor, corporate executive, and in my searching for examples of other holy horizontal calls, I realized another one in two friends of mine, George and Joni B. They are retired, but both have decades of experience as sponsors with both Alcoholics Anonymous (AA) and Al-Anon. I'm amazed at the number of people they serve with the love of Christ. Their service in many ways seems like a full-time occupation. It is most definitely a holy calling.

George shared, "I have a calling, and God rescued me from the pit, and He called me to help others climb out of the pit." And Joni chimed in, "I have the freedom to be a Christian . . . and joy should manifest itself . . . we're supposed to be bright." George followed, "I think in all vocations Christians should act like they believe God and follow the Ten Commandments . . . [and be] a witness to Christ. . . . People see these things and want to know how you do that. . . . We're different people [now and what] is done is not done by me but through Christ." Joni also shared her philosophy by giving me an example of what she said to someone who was once rejecting her. She came back to them with, "I don't need permission to love you."[351]

She also warned, "Blending AA with Christianity . . . is a huge mistake. . . . AA is for sobriety, Al-Anon is for sanity, but the Church is for my soul . . . mixing doesn't work."[352] Both George and Joni—by the grace of God—are keeping the estates distinct, and all the while, love for neighbors is running through their service.

Freed to View Work Differently

As the baptized into Christ, the Christian may view his or her work in a new light:

---

351   George and Joni B., live interview by author, Zoom video call, June 26, 2022.

352   B., interview.

1. Christ makes our work one of our horizontal calls. It is therefore holy, and its status does not depend on human perception, not even our own.

2. Christ places us to shine His light upon a work environment confronted by the world's darkness, and the light in the Christian is greater than that darkness.

3. Christ has given His life and offers new light to those the Christian works for and works with. The Christian is strategically placed to share Christ's light to his neighbor in order that his neighbor might see the unconditional love of Christ.

4. Christ permits a cross upon the Christian through her work. When understood correctly, this cross is used by God to cause us to learn to depend upon the Lord more, not less. In this way, faith in Christ is increased as the flesh is crucified.

5. Christ reminds us that we do not see what we want to see at work, but He also reminds us that we walk by faith and not by sight.

We are now set free from viewing work as drudgery or as a curse. The frustration, of course, will remain. However, Veith reminds us that there is, of course, both blessing *and* curse, but "[w]ith the curse, though, came the promise that the Seed of the woman would crush the Serpent under His feet" (Genesis 3:15), so that now, "the Christian, walking by faith and resting in Christ, can live and work as a channel for the gifts of God."[353]

With the vertical call of Christ for us as baptized children of God, and living in all the estates through the spiritual estate of love for the neighbor, Christ has changed everything so that even in our work—and the *way* in which Christians work—the light of Christ still shines in this world. The crosses will be there, but God will use them to make us stronger, falling into Christ's arms more often and loving our neighbors with increased determination.

---

353   Veith, *God at Work*, 63, 65.

CHAPTER 12 DISCUSSION GUIDE

Christ's Light through Citizens in the Greater Culture

UNCOVER INFORMATION

1. Why are teachers so important to us?

2. Are families and churches also supposed to educate? If so, how?

3. What did C. S. Lewis argue for in respect to good education?

4. List examples of being light in the state through the entertainment industry.

5. How important is work according to God?

DISCOVER MEANING

1. What does *educatio* mean?

2. How did Luther admonish the city council?

3. What did C. S. Lewis say would lead to the abolition of man?

4. What do we mean by "Christ is worthy of receiving all our might"?

5. How is work a form of worshiping God?

EXPLORE IMPLICATIONS

1. What do the best teachers do in relation to their students?

2. What does the "city's best and greatest welfare, safety, and strength" consist of?

3. Why is being a student a calling?

4. How are Christians just like non-Christians in their callings, but also different?

5. What can work do against radical individualism?

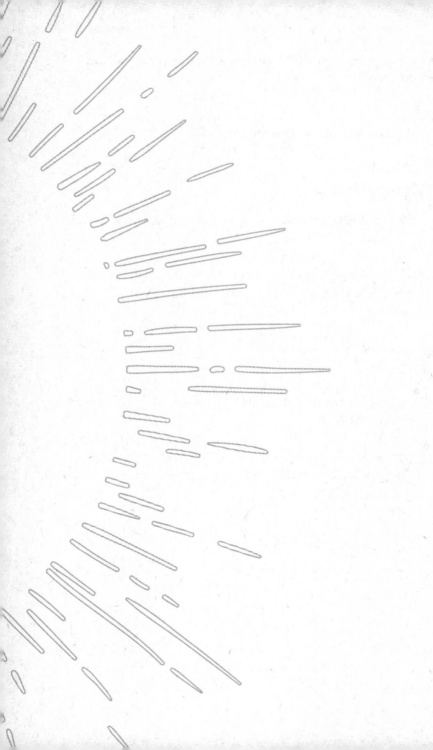

CONCLUSION

SAVING SANCTIFICATION

I shared in the preface that I had been looking for the new life, the life of transformation in all the wrong places. The irony was that I was so busy looking inwardly that I forgot to look up and out toward the neighbor in front of me.

The Lord teaches us plainly, "Anyone who does not love does not know God, because God is love" (1 John 4:8). Relationship is a non-negotiable component in any expression of true love. Where there is not more than one, love cannot exist.

God is love and relationship abounds. The Father loves the Son, the Son loves the Father, and the Holy Spirit is the love that flows between the Father and the Son. The Holy Spirit loves so much that He does not proclaim Himself, but He brings to people the words of Jesus (John 14:26) and then, of course, glory to the Father. His love abounds and because He *is* love, He could not keep it to Himself. He created us in love, and He redeemed us in love. When we chose to turn away from Him, He loved us anyway when He sent Christ. And He loves us now. Love overflows in and through God. Yes, God *is* love.

Jesus showed us the greatest love, laying down His life for us (John 15:13) and all sinners. His was and is the greatest love the world has ever known. While we were weak, ungodly, sinners, and enemies of God, He died for us so that we might be reconciled to God (Romans 5:6–10). Through faith in Christ, we are.

So, sanctification is saved—or its proper meaning protected and perpetuated—through non-concern about our own spiritual lives and the proper preoccupation with our neighbors. Sanctification is saved—better said, *happens*—in and through our holy horizontal calls. And sanctification is created and empowered by our vertical call when God calls us in Christ to be His children baptized into His name.

There is no time-lapse between our being declared righteous, forgiven on account of Christ through faith in Him (*justification*), and our transformed new lives (*sanctification*), but there is a biblical, theological, and logical order: receiving God's call from above and His light from above coming down upon us through His Word and Sacraments *must* come "first" in the biblical, theological, and logical sense. It is not until we are wrapped in Jesus through Baptism and living in His love for us that we are transformed for sanctification, which always expresses itself in love for our neighbor.

This truth has humongous real-life ramifications. God has not called us to be closer to Him on account of our trying to make ourselves holy. He has already made us holy in His Son. So, the life of sanctification is a journey of expressing our joy and thanksgiving and faithfulness to Him by loving our neighbors with no strings attached. "We love because He first loved us" (1 John 4:19). Loving our neighbor is like saying "Amen" to what God has already made us to be in Christ.

Christ Is Always before Us

Jesus makes it lucid for us: "If anyone says, 'I love God,' and hates his brother, he is a liar; for he who does not love his brother whom he has seen cannot love God whom he has not seen. And this commandment we have from him: whoever loves God must also love his brother" (1 John 4:20–21). The one we see before us is God in a mask. It is Jesus in a mask.[354]

Someone might object: "How can you call the terrible sinner in front of me 'Jesus in a mask'?" We can give answer, "Just as easily as I can call *you* Jesus in a mask, because both your sin and your neighbor's sin were put on Jesus" (2 Corinthians 5:21).

---

354   We do not deny that the non-Christian is not yet in holy vocation through faith but "only" in a station in whatever capacity you know them as neighbor. The point here is that we would love all as our Savior did when He died for all.

That is to say that living in our horizontal calls means that not only are *we* a mask of God as we serve our neighbor but with eyes of faith we see Christ in our neighbor. God's way has not changed. He sent His only Son, who humbled Himself by taking on human flesh. In a way, He is still humbling Himself. His mode of operation hasn't changed.

When the Lord Jesus confronted St. Paul when he was Saul on the Damascus road (Acts 9:1–5), Jesus said, "Saul, Saul, why are you persecuting Me?" (Acts 9:4). Saul had been persecuting the Lord's *people*. To God, there was no difference. Thus, at the last judgment Jesus will say to us all, "Truly, I say to you, as you did it to one of the least of these My brothers, you did it to Me" (Matthew 25:40).

Still, in all the cases I've cited above, doesn't it seem apparent that those we are loving are Christians? At 1 John 4:21, we are to love the *brother* who we see. In Acts 9, Jesus refers to Himself as the Church, His Body, exactly the ones Saul had been persecuting. And finally at Matthew 25:40, Jesus says, *"My brothers."*

So, what of the unbeliever, especially that obnoxious one who makes my life miserable, who we know for a fact—because they've made it known—is *not* a Christian? To answer this, we go back to what we've said previously: the one who loves lays down His life for His friends, and (not *but*) Jesus died for us while we were His enemies (Romans 5:10).

In other words, our love is not to follow our judgment and evaluation as to whether anyone is worthy or qualified for our love. No, one way of understanding the Gospel is that Jesus had decided to call enemies friends and unbelievers His people. Hosea 1:10 says: "And in the place where it was said to them, 'You are not My people,' it shall be said to them, 'Children of the living God.'"

We know the saying "Never judge a book by its cover," so we should proceed as if all are one like *the* One, Jesus, no exceptions. And we should know by now: the Lord is quite simply in the business of loving sinners (Matthew 9:13). In our calls, we get to serve them too, just like the King of the Universe served us, the sinners we see in the mirror.

What a great honor we have. Now that we have been made the children of God through His great call, putting us into Christ, Christ's light is now upon us! What a joyful privilege we have. We are set free to share the light of Christ with others in all our horizontal calls. And what a holy arena we have: we get to shine Christ's light in the family, the church, and the state even as members of the spiritual estate where we serve as spiritual priests who love in God's stead.

BIBLIOGRAPHY

Badcock, Gary D. *The Way of Life: A Theology of Christian Vocation*. Grand Rapids, MI: William B. Eerdmans, 1998.

Bonhoeffer, Dietrich. *Life Together*. Translated by John W. Doberstein. New York: Harper Collins, 1954.

Brown, Francis. *The New Brown-Driver-Briggs-Gesenius Hebrew and English Lexicon: With an Appendix Containing the Biblical Aramaic*. Peabody, MA: Hendrickson, 1979.

Carver, Matthew, trans. *Lutheran Prayer Companion*. St. Louis: Concordia Publishing House, 2018.

Chapman, Gary. *The Five Love Languages: The Secret to Love That Lasts*. Chicago: Northfield Publishing, 1992.

Concordia: The Lutheran Confessions. 2nd ed. St. Louis: Concordia Publishing House, 2006.

Espinosa, Alfonso. *Faith That Engages the Culture*. St. Louis: Concordia Publishing House, 2021.

———. *Faith That Sees through the Culture*. St. Louis: Concordia Publishing House, 2018.

Friedrich, Gerhard, and Geoffrey W. Bromiley, eds. *Theological Dictionary of the New Testament*. Translated by Geoffrey W. Bromiley. Vol. 9. Grand Rapids, MI: William B. Eerdmans, 1974.

Gibbs, Jeffrey A. *Matthew 1:1–11:1*. Concordia Commentary. St. Louis: Concordia Publishing House, 2006.

———. *Matthew 11:2–20:34*. Concordia Commentary. St. Louis: Concordia Publishing House, 2010.

Hamburger, Philip. *Separation of Church and State*. Cambridge, MA: Harvard University Press, 2002.

Johnson, Marshall D., ed. *Day by Day We Magnify You: Selected from the Writings of Martin Luther*. Minneapolis: Augsburg Books and Epworth Press, 2008.

Just, Arthur A., Jr. *Luke 1:1–9:50*. Concordia Commentary. St. Louis: Concordia Publishing House, 1996.

Keil, C. F., and F. Delitzsch. *The Pentateuch*. Vol. 3. Biblical Commentary on the Old Testament. Translated by James Martin. Grand Rapids, MI: William B. Eerdmans, n.d.

Keller, Timothy. *The Prodigal God: Recovering the Heart of the Christian Faith*. New York: Dutton, 2008.

Keller, Timothy, and Kathy Keller. *The Meaning of Marriage: Facing the Complexities of Commitment with the Wisdom of God*. New York: Dutton, 2011.

Kittel, Gerhard, and Geoffrey W. Bromiley, eds. *Theological Dictionary of the New Testament*. Translated by Geoffrey W. Bromiley. Vol. 3. Grand Rapids, MI: William B. Eerdmans, 1965.

Kleinig, John W. *Hebrews*. Concordia Commentary. St. Louis: Concordia Publishing House, 2017.

Koester, Craig R. *Symbolism in the Fourth Gospel: Meaning, Mystery, Community*. 2nd ed. Minneapolis: Augsburg Fortress, 2003.

Laetsch, Theo. *Commentary on the Minor Prophets*. St. Louis: Concordia Publishing House, 1956.

Lenski, R. C. H. *The Interpretation of I and II Peter, the Three Epistles of John, and the Epistle of Jude*. Minneapolis: Augsburg, 1966.

———. *The Interpretation of St. John's Gospel*. Minneapolis: Augsburg, 1943.

———. *The Interpretation of St. Luke's Gospel*. Minneapolis: Augsburg, 1946.

———. *The Interpretation of St. Matthew's Gospel*. Minneapolis: Augsburg, 1943.

———. *The Interpretation of St. Paul's Epistles to the Galatians, to the Ephesians and to the Philippians*. Minneapolis: Augsburg, 1937.

Lessing, R. Reed. *Isaiah 40–55*. Concordia Commentary. St. Louis: Concordia Publishing House, 2011.

———. *Isaiah 56–66*. Concordia Commentary. St. Louis: Concordia Publishing House, 2014.

Leupold, H. C. *Exposition of Psalms*. Grand Rapids, MI: Baker Book House, 1959.

Lewis, C. S. *The Abolition of Man: How Education Develops Man's Sense of Morality*. New York: MacMillan, 1947.

———. *The Great Divorce*. New York: MacMillan, 1946.

———. *The Weight of Glory and Other Addresses*. New York: MacMillan, 1949.

Lockwood, Gregory J. *1 Corinthians*. Concordia Commentary. St. Louis: Concordia Publishing House, 2000.

Luther, Martin. *Career of the Reformer: I*. Vol. 31 of *Luther's Works*, American Edition, edited by Harold J. Grimm and Helmut T. Lehmann. Philadelphia: Fortress Press, 1957.

———. *Career of the Reformer: III*. Vol. 33 of *Luther's Works*, American Edition, edited by Philip S. Watson and Helmut T. Lehmann. Philadelphia: Fortress Press, 1972.

———. *Church and Ministry: II*. Vol. 40 of *Luther's Works*, American Edition, edited by Conrad Bergendoff and Helmut T. Lehmann. Philadelphia: Fortress Press, 1958.

———. *Church Postil: II*. Vol. 76 of *Luther's Works*, American Edition, edited by Benjamin T. G. Mayes and James L. Langebartels. St. Louis: Concordia Publishing House, 2013.

———. *Day by Day We Magnify You: Selected from the Writings of Martin Luther*. Edited by Marshall D. Johnson. Minneapolis: Augsburg Books and Epworth Press, 2008.

———. *Devotional Writings: I*. Vol. 42 of *Luther's Works*, American Edition, edited by Martin O. Dietrich and Helmut T. Lehmann. Philadelphia: Fortress Press, 1969.

———. *Lectures on Galatians* (1535) Vol. 26 of *Luther's Works*, American Edition, edited by Jaroslav Pelikan and Walter A. Hansen. St. Louis: Concordia Publishing House, 1963.

———. *Lectures on Isaiah*. Vol. 17 of *Luther's Works*, American Edition, edited by Hilton C. Oswald. St. Louis: Concordia Publishing House, 1972.

———. *Notes on Ecclesiastes; Lectures on the Song of Solomon; Treatise on the Last Words of David*. Vol. 15 of *Luther's Works*, American Edition, edited by Jaroslav Pelikan and Hilton C. Oswald. St. Louis: Concordia Publishing House, 1972.

———. *Selected Psalms: I*. Vol. 12 of *Luther's Works*, American Edition, edited by Jaroslav Pelikan. St. Louis: Concordia Publishing House, 1955.

———. *Selected Psalms: III*. Vol. 14 of *Luther's Works*, American Edition, edited by Jaroslav Pelikan and Daniel E. Poellot. St. Louis: Concordia Publishing House, 1958.

———. *Sermons: I*. Vol. 51 of *Luther's Works*, American Edition, edited by John W. Doberstein and Helmut T. Lehmann. Translated by John W. Doberstein. Philadelphia: Fortress Press, 1959.

———. *The Christian in Society: I*. Vol. 44 of *Luther's Works*, American Edition, edited by James Atkinson and Helmut T. Lehmann. Philadelphia: Fortress Press, 1966.

———. *The Christians in Society: II*. Vol. 45 of *Luther's Works*, American Edition, edited by Walther I. Brandt and Helmut T. Lehmann. Philadelphia: Fortress Press, 1962.

———. *The Sermons on the Mount (Sermons) and the Magnificat*. Vol. 21 of *Luther's Works*, American Edition, edited by Jaroslav Pelikan. St. Louis: Concordia Publishing House, 1956.

———. *Word and Sacrament: I*. Vol. 35 of *Luther's Works*, American Edition, edited by E. Theodore Bachman and Helmut T. Lehmann. Philadelphia: Fortress Press, 1960.

———. *Word and Sacrament: III*. Vol. 37 of *Luther's Works*, American Edition, edited by Robert H. Fischer and Helmut T. Lehmann. Philadelphia: Fortress Press, 1961.

Middendorf, Michael P. *Romans 1–8*. Concordia Commentary. St. Louis: Concordia Publishing House, 2013.

———. *Romans 9–16*. Concordia Commentary. St. Louis: Concordia Publishing House, 2016.

Oswalt, John N. *The New International Commentary on the Old Testament*. Grand Rapids, MI: William B. Eerdmans, 1986.

Peters, Albrecht. *Commentary on Luther's Catechisms: Confession and Christian Life*. St. Louis: Concordia Publishing House, 2013.

Rest, Friedrich. *Our Christian Symbols*. Cleveland, OH: The Pilgrim Press, 1954.

Scaer, David P. *The Sermon on the Mount: The Church's First Statement of the Gospel*. St. Louis: Concordia Publishing House, 2000.

Schaff, Philip. *History of the Christian Church*, Vol. 1. Peabody, MA: Hendrickson, 1858.

Smith, Gary Scott. *Faith and the Presidency: From George Washington to George W. Bush*. New York: Oxford University Press, 2006.

The Lutheran Church—Missouri Synod. *Confession and Absolution: A Report of the Commission on Theology and Church Relations*. St. Louis: The Lutheran Church—Missouri Synod, 2018.

The Lutheran Church—Missouri Synod. *Lutheran Service Book: Agenda*. St. Louis: Concordia Publishing House, 2006.

Tocqueville, Alexis de. *Democracy in America*. Abridged by Sanford Kessler. Translated by Stephen D. Grant. Indianapolis: Hackett, 2000.

Uhlhorn, Gerhard. *Christian Charity in the Ancient Church*. Translated by Matthew C. Harrison. New York: Charles Scribner's Sons, 1883.

Veith, Gene Edward, Jr. *God at Work: Your Christian Vocation in All of Life*. Wheaton, IL: Crossway Books, 2002.

Volf, Miroslav, and Ryan McAnnally-Linz. *Public Faith in Action: How to Engage with Commitment, Conviction, and Courage*. Grand Rapids, MI: Brazos Press, 2016.

Webb-Mitchell, Brett P. *Christly Gestures: Learning to Be Members of the Body of Christ*. Grand Rapids, MI: William B. Eerdmans, 2003.

Weinrich, William C. *John 1:1–7:1*. Concordia Commentary. St. Louis: Concordia Publishing House, 2015.

Winger, Thomas M. *Ephesians*. Concordia Commentary. St. Louis: Concordia Publishing House, 2015.

Wingren, Gustaf. *Luther on Vocation*. Translated by Carl C. Rasmussen. Eugene, OR: Wipf and Stock, 1957.

TOPICAL INDEX

SCRIPTURAL INDEX